D1378103

DIVINITY SPEAKS

WOMEN WHO TUNE IN & TRUST DIVINE INSPIRATION

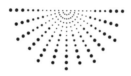

ABIGAIL HINDS   ALYSEMARIE GALLAGHER WARREN

AMANDA RUMORE   ANDREA BLINDT

ANNELISA VALLERY   ASHLEY ABRAMSON

BRANDY KNIGHT   CAROL LOUISE SCHOFFMANN

ELISHA GREENLEAF   EMILY REIMANN

HEATHER O'NEILL   HEATHER ROBINSON

HOLLY BUHLER   JESS HOEPER   JUDIE HURTADO

JULIE AIRD   LINSEY MOSES SMITH

MARDALENA DAWN TURPEL   MELISSA LAMBOUR

NICOLE HANLON REID   SUZANNE NICHOLE PRESTON

TAMMY BRASWELL   TARA HAISLIP

TERA NAMDEEP KAUR   TISH MEEHAN

EXALTED PUBLISHING HOUSE

CONTENTS

INTRODUCTION

Divinity is defined as "the quality or state of being divine."

What do you think about when you hear the word "Divinity"?

Do you hear the church bells ringing?

The memories of talking to your Spirit Guides as a child?

A strong sense, an inner-knowing, a trust in the unseen?

What does it *stir* up within you?

If you were to have asked me years ago what the word "*Divinity*" means to me, I probably would have scoffed and said, "yeah–that's not for me."

But through a series of beautiful, divine, raw, real, human events–the spiritual path chose me. A path to help me understand myself, my existence and my place on this precious planet.

DIVINITY

Now, the sight of those eight letters makes me feel something powerful.

A sense of peace.

A sense of connection.

A knowingness of something greater.

Many years ago, a book called "Autobiography of a Yogi" by Paramahansa Yogananda fell into my lap. This book opened my eyes even wider to the spiritual landscape as well as the many ways we can connect with God and those who have come here to be bearers of this truth. It brought me home to Love.

"God is Love; His plan for creation can be rooted only in love. Does not that simple thought, rather than erudite reasonings, offer solace to the human heart? Every saint who has penetrated to the core of Reality has testified that a divine universal plan exists and that it is beautiful and full of joy."

— PARAMAHANSA YOGANANDA

Personally, I was brought up in a Catholic family and thought that going to church on Sunday mornings was the only path to God. I dreaded the weekly CCD (Confraternity of Christian Doctrine) classes feeling like there had to be more to this God conversation. The teachings felt stale, the stories didn't hit home and I couldn't understand how to put the words from the Bible into practice.

Looking back, it feels like a *Cosmic Haha* since the seeds of Divinity were planted at a very young age, but I wasn't ready to see them and I needed to have an understanding of this work in my own way. Now, I feel more connected to God, Source, Spirit, Universe and the Divine than ever before. I am able to see the beautiful thread through all religions, spiritual practices, metaphysical teachings and feel that they are all connecting us back to Love, just through different stories, language and perspectives.

Oh, *how beautiful*.

So what is Divinity Speaks?

This is truly a book about *finding your way home*.

Be it through God, connecting to your physical body or finally listening to the messages that Source has been trying to whisper (or maybe *yell*) at you.

I wanted to hear about the many ways that women tune in and trust their own source of *Divine Inspiration,* may it be through nature, a religion, a feeling, a knowingness, or something else.

It felt like it was time to share with the world the many ways that we are able to be, do, live and understand our precious lives and relationship to something greater on the planet.

You may refer to this Divinity as Source, Spirit, the Universe, God, your Spirit Guides or something else.

Each chapter represents a different perspective on how you can come back home to yourself.

To find and feel peace.

To learn and unlearn.

To see and to be seen.

To feel worthy, loved and supported.

We are living in a day and age where there is more than one way to do anything.

There's not just one right way to your career success.

There's not just one right way to build a business.

There's not just one right way to have a healthy relationship.

There's not just one right way to heal your body.

Within these pages, you will see the many unique ways to understand, navigate, approach and be with the divinity that speaks through you.

Enjoy the journey back home to yourself.

And remember to listen to the divine inspiration that flows through you in each moment.

- Bridget Aileen Sicsko

THE FEMININE WELL

ABIGAIL HINDS

THE DEEP WELL OF FEMININE INTELLIGENCE

*W*e all have an inner well of feminine intelligence. A fountain eternally flowing with guidance and wisdom, resource and belonging.

The medicine from this well of the feminine flows from the source of life itself. The womb of the great mother. This is where magic lives. This is the place where we encounter our sixth sense, our deeper sense, and all of our senses beyond that. It is the place of our innate and primal knowing and unknowing.

The intelligence that springs from this deep well of the feminine is beyond what could ever be created through the mind. It is beyond the confines of logic, and limitations of linear thought. It is through our bodies that we receive the feminine intelligence of life.

THE SEVERANCE

There has been a programming. A domestication. A disconnection from the wild waters of this inner fountain. A severance from the nourishment of this feminine flow. This trickster coding has made us believe we are in an inner and outer drought. That there is no well to drink from. Dry. Depleted. Parched. Separate. Alone. Isolated. Endlessly searching for something outside of ourselves to quench this primal thirst. Never satiated.

The pathways for how to tap into this feminine well have been long forgotten. They were left out of our educational curriculums. They were burned and buried, boarded up, and hidden away long ago. People do not even remember that there ever was a well. "That's nonsense!" they say. "I have never seen the well. I have never drank from such a place. It must not exist!"

What a twisted story. Because, you see, we are the well. It is encoded in the very cells of our being to be in connection with this ever flowing fountain. Always available to us. Always beckoning us home.

Disconnection from this feminine well, is disconnection from life itself.

The constructions of this modern world, born exclusively from the mind, brings us further away from this feminine intelligence. Further away from our direct communication with the most primal intelligence of life.

Just look around... at the so-called 'progress' of our modern creations. Skyscrapers of metal and glass, filled with little square boxes, towering high over mazes of concrete. Cars buzzing, humming, speeding in this direction and that, moving fast fast fast. Trees cut down en masse, or existing within manicured tiny little squares of dirt. Pavement blanketing the earth like a frozen hard river. Our feet squished and suffocating in plastic shoes, thumping hard and unforgiving concrete slabs. Our roots, floating as little dangles, barely able to touch any earth. Our bodies rushing around, following our heads from here to there in a stressful flurry.

All of this is fueled by the extraction and degradation of our Mother Earth. Of the wild and natural places. The indigenous communities. All of this is foundationally built on the disconnection and dishonoring of the source of life.

This is not true progress. This is delusion and destruction. Extraction and greed. This is the way of wounded children who are disconnected from the pulsing heart of their Mother. This is the way of those who have forgotten the nourishment of the feminine well.

We have forgotten our roots of connection to life.

MY WOMB STORY

I will share some of my womb story, and how I was pulled down into this feminine well.

I grew up completely disconnected from my womb. I would only really pay attention to her that first day of my bleeding every month, when she screamed out in agony and pain. Like clockwork, every cycle, I would go to the nurse at school and ask to go home early. I would curl up in my bed with a hot pack and wait for the advil to kick in and bring some relief. My womb was trying to speak to me. Screaming to get my attention, but I didn't know how to listen.

The thought I have now, of having to go to school while I am bleeding - sitting still in an uncomfortable chair, taking in endless hours of information and talking, interacting with tons of other kids - that sounds absolutely insane. During the bleeding time, the body is in a profound ceremony – blood is literally flowing as a river out of the yoni. It is not a time to drive a car, or lift heavy weights, or sit in a crowded room. It is a time to rest and rejuvenate, to listen deeply and receive.

The fact that wombed ones are expected to go to school/work/events while they are bleeding is a stark example of how little the womb is understood and respected in these modern times.

See, the womb is an Oracle. Especially during the bleeding time. There is a unique portal that opens, where we have more access to the whispers of spirit and messages from the magical ones that live beyond the veils of normal reality. We have deeper access to the dreaming dragon womb of Mother Earth. This time was and still is valued deeply in many indigenous cultures. Women would bring back prophecies and messages that could support the survival and thriving of the entire village. This is the potential potency of the bleeding time. A prophetic and deeply spiritual experience.

Anyone with a womb knows this experience of being pulled down into the body – into this deeper and slower place. This place can feel very unfamiliar and even terrifying, as we are often used to living up, above, in the mind, in the future, and in fast paced everything.

The bleeding time drops you down into this deep feminine well. It is true that if we are not used to inhabiting this place, we may need to face what we have been avoiding, what has been lurking in the darkness. What has been silenced and neglected. This can be an ugly and deeply disturbing process. It can also be wildly beautiful, even ecstatic. Likely some of all of it will come through. This is a place where we find our deepest terrors. It is also a place where we discover the magic and medicine we carry.

In the structure of this modern matrix, so many wombed ones must push forward into all 'normal' activities and never get to drop into the true medicine of our bleeding time. We have largely forgotten the magic of the womb.

GOING DEEPER

I went through a deep initiatory experience with my bleeding time that radically shifted my relationship and innerstanding to this special time.

During a tumultuous time in my twenties, I spent a month in solitary confinement in Jail. That experience is a whole other story, for another time. The point of me mentioning it here though, is because it was the first time in my life that I was completely by myself for the duration of my bleeding time. Completely alone inside a concrete box.

Leading up to this experience, I had been moving so very fast, my schedule was completely full, and I was running around exhausted and burnt out without even realizing it. So this halt in everything felt abrupt and intense. No events to go to, no friends, no phone, no wifi, no books, no snacks, no tea, no music. Just. With. Myself.

And then, two weeks in, my bleeding time came. It was just me and my womb. Nowhere to go, no ways to distract, no comforts or resources.

At the time, I was already attuned to my womb cycle to some degree, and would give myself extra space and rest and nourishment during my bleeding time. But in this modern age, actual true rest and four whole days alone never seemed to happen, not even close.

The beginning was riding out waves and waves of pulsing pain. Dancing, shaking, touching, breathing into places I had never actually contacted before, always ran away from. I had to channel and move the energy. I cried and raged and went through a deep emotional cleansing for days. It felt like long pent up feelings were flowing out of me as rivers of tears, and spewing out of me as bursts of raging flame.

After I moved through the very intense waves of this experience, my system eventually began to settle and rest and became more still and empty. There was a lot of profound nothingness, staring off into space, immersed in the void. And around day four, after the wild dragon ride, I began to have some of the most mystical experiences I ever had. I channeled a whole amazing song about a spider and weaving. It just flowed through me, naturally. I had my first encounter with one of my spirit guides who began teaching me things and sharing messages with me. This kind of magic had not been happening or accessible to me in such a way before this experience. I had been more full of self-doubt and low self-esteem to believe this could be possible for me. I had also been moving too fast and too much in my mind to even have the space to listen and receive this kind of magic.

These magical experiences began opening because I was actually present and connecting with my womb. I was forced to face her pain and be with it. To ride on its waves and listen, rather than make it go away or distract myself so I could get on with things as usual.

The womb begins to speak when we make space to listen.

WOMB AWAKENING

Back in 2012, I was in my early twenties, fresh out of college. After a series of wild synchronicities and traumatic events, I was led to my first Acupuncture appointment. The traumatic events I had been through left me recovering from a kidney infection, and in immense discomfort and pain from a copper IUD they had inserted. These experiences began to clearly reveal to me the ways in which the modern medical system was severely lacking in capacity to support women's health. How this system can actually cause more trauma and suffering. This revelation continued throughout my journey as I dove into the field of womb and breast health, where the systems of modern gynecology and 'women's health' are sorely inadequate, uneducated and outdated.

Amazingly, for this first alternative medicine session of my life, I found myself in the gorgeous and serene space of an incredibly magical, highly skilled and powerful woman. From the moment I came into the space it felt like I was in another realm that evoked a certain peacefulness and beauty of spirit. That evoked the feeling of true health and balance. She had me fill out an intake form, and I immediately noted with curiosity and concern that the questions she asked me were so much more thorough than any doctor had asked me before. I had gone to doctors all throughout my life, and was used to a short and surface level visit, them asking a thing or two, taking my blood pressure and saying "Great! You seem super healthy. All is good". This was the first time that meeting with a health practitioner felt like an actual authentic investigation into what was going on with my body and health.

When I was with her and going over the questions, she asked me, "Where are you at in your cycle?", "What cycle?" I replied. I didn't even know what she meant. She then explained that those with a womb have four distinct phases of their monthly cycle. It's not just menstruation, each phase of the cycle is unique and has the body in a different configuration of hormones and experience. She was asking because she said that depending on where I was in my cycle, I may need slightly different treatment.

She recommended the book 'Taking Charge of Your Fertility' by Toni Weschler that described the cycles of the womb and learning to track them so you can identify where you are at in your cycle. I was completely blown away. In awe. It was like learning some long lost secret key to my own body. This is what is really going on?! I am a cyclical being! It explained so much. I also felt upset, frustrated and confused, wondering "why didn't I learn about all this in middle school?" It seemed like such basic and fundamental information about my body and the experience of having a womb.

I also had my IUD taken out right away. This healer didn't directly tell me to do so, but she did tell me that in Chinese Medicine an IUD is referred to as something like "metal intrusion in the uterus". Also that I was still in pain because my cervix was inflamed from this unnatural object, and that it was not healthy or natural to walk around with an inflamed cervix for seven months (though my doctor told me this was "perfectly normal" and nothing to worry about). That was enough information for me. As I listened, maybe for the first time ever, my womb communicated a clear "f*ck no, get this thing out of me". It became obvious that this foreign object causing pain in my womb was NOT supporting my body.

This began my journey of listening to the voice of my womb.

The path of the womb is a path of the soul. A path of returning home to the feminine well of medicine and magic. In walking this womb path, I have learned to trust the voice of my womb and my body as my greatest navigation system. As my way to live my life from the call of my own wild soul, from the call of the Earth and Spirit. Rather than a programmed way that is of someone else's agenda, serving a purpose I don't stand behind or believe in.

I walk continually spiraling into deeper connection with the web of life, deeper connection to my body, deeper connection to the mother, deeper connection to the feminine well of nourishment.

Yet, this has not been an easy journey. For we are mending generations of this great separation from the feminine well. Parts of my womb journey have been deeply tumultuous, confusing, disorienting, and terrifying. Connecting to this place has brought up buried experiences, abusive relationships, and times of my life when this space had been violated and disrespected. Through my womb connection, I began to touch into the ancestral womb wounds of my female lineage. The generations of disconnection are real, and felt within my own body.

Through this path I also began to uncover the great disconnection from this sacred space that lives in the collective. I realized it was not just in me, but in wombed ones all around me, and in the greater architecture of our entire society.

As I sat in women's circles, red tents, womb workshops; I realized that most of us in the modern world had grown up in this disconnection. Not being initiated into the incredible spiritual power and technology residing within our own bodies. Thinking that p*ssy is 'weak' and our blood is 'gross', and our creative center is something to sell for sexual attention, or hide in shame. The true power and potency of the life-giving powers of creation, shrouded in layers of shame and trauma. Hidden and shunned away by generations upon generations of survival and protection.

Disrespect and disregard for this sacred space, is disrespect and disregard for life itself. The sacredness of life is the sacredness of our wombs.

We are in a great remembering of the womb ways. And the wellspring of the deep feminine intelligence is always flowing. Alive within our own beautiful bodies.

MY DEVOTION TO THE WOMB OF LIFE

I do what I do so that the future generations of women grow up connected to their bodies, feeling the rhythm of the Earth pulsing in their wombs. So that the future generations of women grow up activated in their magical senses of intuition and feminine intelligence. So we may birth our new creations in deep connection to the life-giving powers of the womb, singing the harmonics of right relation with all of creation.

~ Divinity Speaking ~
"Your womb is the source of life. Drop in. "

ABOUT THE AUTHOR
ABIGAIL HINDS

Abigail Hinds is the founder of Whale Womb Weaving, a business focused on nourishing the life-giving powers of the feminine body and soul. Abigail is a Feminine Wisdom Keeper, a Rainbow Medicine Weaver, and an Animal Kin Ambassador.

Through ancient feminine nourishment practices, Abigail supports magically inclined wombed ones to embody their wild feminine roots, awaken their magical compass of intuition, and walk their unique path of soul, all through the temple of the body and rooted deeply in the wisdom ways of the earth.

Abigail has a degree in Art and Architectural studies from Brown University. She has taught feminine wisdom workshops and ceremonies at events and major gatherings across the country, such as Symbiosis, NorCal Permaculture Convergence and Spirit Weavers.

An artist at heart, Abigail enjoys weaving baskets, pendants and feather wands with the medicines of the earth, at her home in the forests of the Pacific Northwest.

Website: www.whalewombweaving.com

Instagram: @whalewombweaving

2

THE MAGIC OF THE UNSPOKEN

ALYSEMARIE GALLAGHER WARREN

I want to start this love letter from the Divine to all of us. These downloads dropped in after I said yes to sharing my story.

1. There is a magic that happens when you surrender to your knowing, the act of fully trusting your own inner compass. Your gut, your heart, your body...they are receptors to a language that goes beyond the words our minds understand. The magic lies in the unspoken language of your intuition. The feeling that courses through your veins when you align with the higher power that guides you. When you accept that you're a beacon — a channel — and that you're on earth to be a receiver and a deliverer of something bigger than yourself.

2. You're never experiencing life alone. I'm not talking about having friends and family. I'm talking about being tapped into infinite Source, God, The Universe, or whatever name you use.

3. Divinity doesn't just channel in words through my mind, it's also in my body: my footsteps are a constant recalibration of the world around me. Divinity is moving through me to you in the ripples that are created with the weight of my body... through the smells that catch my attention...through everything that pulls my focus.

4. During mundane tasks my channel is flooded with what I need or what the world needs in this now. It's me, the world needs me. It's those tasks that allow my mind to wander and get lost in the superhighway of the divine. For some people nature encourages their flow, but not me. I'm distracted by the beauty of nature. It's the daily tasks of my life — cutting vegetables, washing dishes, today making chips — that I relax and allow the flow of divine information to flood every cell of my body.

5. In the past when I channeled, I used to say that I took a step back and let Spirit step in. Now, I understand that my ego is taking a step aside. I needed to let my learned behaviors shift, to make room for the Divine to speak through me and to me. I become more me in those moments. I am able to see the Divine in me. Hear the Divine more clearly. I see my truth with no filter, no human experience between me and all that is divine.

So let me tell you a little story or two about me.

When I was deciding where to go to college, I had a vision of what I wanted. I had an idea of how I wanted to be seen, but deep down I knew that when I found the place I would call home, I would know. We visited schools. I saw the campuses. I met the people. I found a place that felt good enough. I almost said yes. Then, I decided to visit one more place and in my first footsteps, I remember the thought, this is my place. It was small, beautiful...and it was home. I remember someone asking me how I chose it, and telling them, "I just know."

I made a million decisions this way before I ever understood about intuition or the Divine. The one thing that felt sure in my life was that if I listened to my heart everything would work out. I could tell you hundreds of these moments in my life from childhood through college, long before I got to the moments of understanding I have now. A piece of me has always known that my heart had all the answers I needed and that I was meant to be here, now.

In Legacy Speaks, I shared about my moment with Jesus in my bedroom where He told me that I had a purpose and to be His voice. It took a long time for me to understand what that meant, how it worked, or how I could possibly do it. I started sharing my story whenever I felt called. I learned to share honestly about my struggles and be comfortably vulnerable.

However, I stuck to my life experience because anything outside my personal experience seemed like something I had made up. I wasn't ready or able to explain that to anyone because I didn't understand it yet myself.

I have this vivid memory of being at the gym with my mom, sitting around having morning coffee with her friends, and talking with them about hormones in chickens that were affecting young girls. I wasn't sure if it was fact or something

I had heard but I remember my mom looking at me and asking me how I knew so much about this. At that moment I had an inner conversation about knowing. I had no business knowing this information because it was not something I had researched, yet I fully knew that the information came from inside me...and it wasn't bullsh*t! This is my first vivid memory of having a download of information from Source.

I eventually got used to knowing information I had no business knowing. I knew that I knew in my whole being. I went through this thought process time and time again: "Am I making this up? Am I just lying? Am I crazy?" Something inside me pushed me past these doubts to knowing, that everything I knew in those moments were truths that I was receiving from something outside myself.

It wasn't long after this that I started referring to my brain as a filing cabinet of truths. It seemed to always have the answers I needed when I needed them. A few years ago, I finally decided to let go of the notion that this process was crazy. I stepped into believing.

I remember the first time I experienced someone else channeling information from Source. At that moment I realized that she was doing exactly what I was doing! I was tapped in, connected, and being given the words that I needed in the moment that I needed them: this was the beginning!

When I accepted that something I had always wanted was actually true, I was the channel I dreamed of being. I claimed my power. I said "Yes!" I shed the doubts, the what-ifs, the maybes, the some days, and the judgment. I opened myself up to the endless possibility of my authentic truth. The Divine speaks through me and I was finally listening.

Have you heard the phrase when the door closes, a window opens? This is what channeling is for me: a window opening to the things I had only dreamed of...things I know I am worthy of dreaming.

So, what happens when you open the proverbial window? Fresh air comes in and you release stagnant energy. You also get to release feelings of shame and guilt, doubts, old stories, patterns and everything that no longer serve you. You get to make space for the things you've been wanting. Channeling the Divine doesn't only let things in, it lets them out too. Hearing the Divine helps you to understand that you've been given the tools to deal with your human experience, your suffering, your trauma, and your confusion.

For some people it comes in mediation, exercise, sleep, writing, or in signs. There is no right or wrong way to hear the words of the Divine.

For me, channeling happens when I let my guard down. In places like the shower or while I'm cooking, in creation, or sometimes in meditation, but mostly it comes in the mundane moments when I'm open to my own possibilities. I bridge the gap between earth and the space above.

When I tell you that the Divine speaks in all kinds of moments, I mean it. When I open up the space to channel the Divine — a spirit guide, a light being, or a loved one for someone else — the download comes in ways that the receiver is best open to receiving it. So when I'm the receiver, it comes when I'm most open to receiving, when my mind is resting and I least expect it. Most importantly, there is nothing to get in the way of the channel.

Let me tell you about the first time I very confidently channeled for a stranger. A couple of years ago, I was beginning to be open to channeling for others. I received what I call spiritual voicemail for a woman I hadn't met and only dreamed of being friends with. I was so confident that she needed the message that I had for her that I sent her a message. I asked if she would be open to chatting because her spirit guides had come to me. I'd never been so forward or confident about anything like this before, and yet I knew in my whole being that this is what I was supposed to do. She messaged me back and asked if I could talk right then. I was thrilled and excited to share the message with her. We had the longest chat! We opened portals, we laughed, we shared a-ha moments, and she asked me to be on her podcast. More importantly, we became friends. Through me she received the exact message she needed to expand, to grow, to shift, and to push herself into new places.

This is the magic: I listened, even though I was scared. This seemed out of my comfort zone but Spirit had whispered and nudged, and I finally said okay. The magic of that moment was two fold, it was for us both. She received a message her team was dying to share with her and I received the confirmation I needed: the message that I was ready.

I've had many more moments like that one because I started believing that magic was possible! I stopped limiting the Universe by creating expectations and beliefs that had no room for magic.

The Divine doesn't see things like we do. The Divine doesn't judge us, doesn't care about how you look, doesn't have expectations of you. The Divine simply works within the limits you've set or are open to.

When I was a kid I was taught to pray like I was sending a wish list to God. The tricky part about that mentality is that God doesn't see life like we do. The Divine sees the big picture and the limitless possibilities of the unclouded human mind.

Let me show you what happens when you trust and align with the little voice in your head. When you are in control of your thoughts and you understand that you have a choice.

On this particular morning, I woke up feeling 'yucky'. I was in the depths of the place in my mind that feels like a trap: no clear entrance or exit, an endless loop of chaos and doubt. I had already decided that I didn't align with this place anymore and today I decided to deal with it. The Divine triggered my heart, and instead of struggling through a crappy day I felt my whole being say, "F*CK NO!"

I don't choose this.
I don't choose struggle.
I don't choose a crappy day.
I don't choose the back room.
Instead,
I leaned into gratitude.
I love my life.
I have wonderful people around me. I am happy.
I get to choose!

I put on music that lights my soul up. I went into mantra.

I looked at the world around me.

I saw my signs, a cardinal and a hawk. I focused on my breathing.

I am not controlled by my mind, I'm not subject to the darkness,

I don't need the safety of the back room, I don't need the comfort of my sadness...

That is not me anymore. That's an old story.

That's who I was and I'm grateful for her.

But I'm not her anymore. I've come too far.

I've expanded too much.

I'm too magnificent to hide in the back.

I shine too bright to be dimmed by my own doing.

I choose life.

I choose happiness.

I choose joy.

I choose to be seen.

I received this beautiful download of understanding: I had needed the back room for so long, but equally, I no longer needed it. This is what I received, "The back room was safety, because I was the only one allowed in. You have always been your own safety." In this download I realized that survival mode was helping exist in a world where I didn't feel accepted. I created a space where I could tune out the outside noise so I could fully be who I was, just as I was. After healing, blossoming, growing, shifting, and expanding, I no longer needed that kind of safety. I've learned that I can be myself. I've found spaces where I belong and I no longer need to try to fit in. I can always be me.

Because I chose to take back control and listen to the divinity in me, I realized my desire for validation. I needed someone else to validate my worth. I needed you to tell me that my healing had worked, that my food was good, that I was funny... that I was pretty. I only knew I was worthy if it was validated by someone else. Then, I saw a former client thriving.

She was putting out new offerings, glowing like the sun, and I thought, "Man, I wish I knew that I was part of that. I wish she would tell me I helped her." Those thoughts plagued me and made me feel sad. When I realized I had a choice I shifted. I chose to be happy for her and let the Divine in. I knew for myself, in my whole body, that I was a part of it. She didn't need to see it! I was part of it. I didn't need her validation because it's the truth. I was part of her journey. I was a portal to this reality for her, and I get to be proud of her. I get to be proud of us both.

This is how the Divine works, if you let it. It will guide you to the truth, it will lead you to what you need. The Divine will hold you while you begin to understand.

Before I honored my channel, I believed that worthiness was something some people had and you had to earn it. It's what I was taught and how the people around me acted. It's how I learned to be. Worthiness came from those who were worthy and they had to choose you to be worthy, too. Then, you had to work to maintain it. As I type this I'm in tears because I know that much of the world accepts this as true and a lot of people thrive on knowing they are worthy because they have been told they are.

But now, as a channel, as a receiver and a deliverer for the unspoken words of the Divine — as someone who understands her own divinity — I get to tell you: You are worthy just because you are you. You have nothing to earn. You have nothing to prove. No one can take your worthiness away. It's your truth and so it is.

I want you to know that you get to hear and feel the unspoken language of the Divine too. You get to align with the truth that is spoken through you. No matter what it looks like, how it feels, or what language it is, your truth is the truth. With open arms you are received just as you are. You don't have to change. It gets to be easy. It will be just as you desire it to be. The world needs you, it needs the authentic divine being that you are.

Breathe deep,
Feel the warm white light, Open your heart,
Close down your mind, Activate all your senses, And receive,
Because the Divine is always speaking. Are you open to listening?
You're always exactly where you need to be, who you need to be.

~ *Divinity Speaking* ~
"As you were, as you are, as you will be, it's always you. Just you."

ABOUT THE AUTHOR

ALYSEMARIE WARREN

AlyseMarie Warren is a Master healer and the go-to "spiritual sidekick" for high level leaders. She helps high achieving women who have created 6 & 7 figure businesses, to create safe spaces to rest, heal and process their success. AlyseMarie's work is rooted in her connection to Mary Magdalene to provide intuitive guidance while her connection to Mother Gaia allows her to be the grounded, spiritual confidant. AlyseMarie is an Executive Chef in Chicago and lives in a cute eclectic bungalow with her artist husband, Spence, and their cat Kramer.

Website: www.alysemariewarren.com

Instagram: @i.am.alysemarie

3

MOTHERHOOD

AMANDA RUMORE

*W*hat is divinity to you? Initially, I was uncertain of my definition of this enchanting word. Upon meditating for a deeper understanding, I immediately felt that Godliness equals divinity. When I think of Godliness, I think of just that; God, our Father. I wanted to further explore so I closed my eyes and focused on the darkest sky imaginable, and I faintly saw a statue. As I inched closer to this vision, the surrounding enclave, seemingly picturesque, was familiar. With a deep inhale, I smelt the fresh blossoms of the hand-picked bouquets adorning the captivating sculpture of Mother Mary. The glistening of the rosary draped over her clasped hands caught my attention. I was at my daughter's school, where I unintentionally passed this version of the Virgin Mary time and time again.

Growing up Catholic, I am well acquainted with Mother Mary. After having our first daughter, my husband, Anthony and I struggled with fertility. This repeatedly led me to seek out Mary. A few years ago, I felt driven to say the rosary more often, which directed me to her.

Both of my grandmothers have passed, and their endless maternal beauty reminds me of the exquisiteness of Mother Mary.

Speaking of the greatness of my grandmothers, their ethereal maternal strength undeniably saved my life. In July 2018, I fell 40 feet from an energy vortex in Sedona, Arizona. The vortex, Kachina Woman and Warrior Man located in Boynton Canyon, is a notable Sedona landmark, often recognized as the most powerful Sedona vortex and offers deep spirituality and dynamic energy.

Within the canyon walls of these breathtaking majestic mountains, it is so peaceful you can nearly hear a pin drop. Throughout history, many generations, centuries before Columbus, claimed an intense spiritual connection to the Boynton Canyon vortexes. On the left is the massive rock formation named Warrior Man, the masculine energy known to bestow positivity, joy, and rejuvenation. The tall formation on the right is Kachina Woman, the feminine energy that triggers great introspection, leading many to feel more connected to past or lost memories. Both structures together are said to present power in fertility.

During a family hike on that warm summer day, the captivating red rocks gloriously bestow intriguing allure. Although Anthony requested that I skip the trek up Warrior Man, I ignored his plea and proceeded. Although we had been there before and hiked this exact route, at that moment I was explicitly drawn to this addictive energy. The previous day, I experienced my first-ever energy reading and confidently felt both grandmothers beside me, still nestling my hands. Indisputably, I was meant for that journey that day, and nothing would stop me.

After reaching the peak and waving to my then 4-year-old-daughter, Mia Valentina, showing her some of our favorite yoga poses, I began my descent down the steep energy vortex. My footing became weaker as I searched for a poised backstep.

Darkness. Silence.

Sirens. Blades.

I didn't know it yet, but both grandmothers, Helen and Valentine, did save me on that fateful day. The science behind my fall and the magnitude of my recovery still don't make sense. I should not have lived after the agonizing plunge. My recovery should have been filled with even more hardship. While hospitalized with a traumatic brain injury, cracked vertebrae, broken arm, and no understanding of how to walk, I constantly told everyone who would listen that these women – my angels – saved me.   In the first days, I couldn't remember my name or age, yet I knew my grandmothers wrapped their spirits around my body to protect me and ensure vitality. They provided divine intervention. I still have no memory from those days, but I am told that I talked to both of my grandmothers and great-grandmother, Pearl, from my hospital bed. **At my purest time, I understood divinity.**

Eventually, I am transported to a second hospital, where I lived in a more conscious state. Besides constantly praising God for his grace, I become very vocal about my desire, my instinctual need, in having more children. Motherhood is far past important to me, rather it is critical to my existence. I am unable to manage the most mundane tasks and often believe I am a child living in my parent's house, yet my drive to further my family line was unapologetically demanding. When leaving the hospital to finally return home, I ask my medical team three questions:

1. Can I drive?
2. Can I have more children?
3. Can I write?

Nobody could answer me.

In my most natural state, I viewed motherhood as ultimate divinity. My mom flew 2,000 miles the day of my accident, and drove another 2 hours, to ensure she was next to me as I battled life versus death. I am the oldest of her five children, and my mom still moves mountains for us. Unbeknownst to me, my youngest sister drives 250 miles through the mountains, amongst torrential rains in the darkest night sky, so she can sit next to me and brush my matted, blood filled hair. I didn't realize then, but one of my closest friends stayed next to me for days. She dropped her life and left her family – husband and two small children – and drove hours to be with me and my family during this time of tragedy. Although unconscious, they demonstrated the divinity of motherhood to me.

When I returned home after a month-long hospital stay, I fiercely fought to be a mother once again to my daughter. I could barely bathe myself, but I sat with Mia during her bath time. I could not yet make an actual meal, but I made her lunch for preschool. I can't yet read or write, but together we read, colored, and played games. Although I am not able to drive, I accompanied Anthony on his daily drives to her school. I don't realize it but the foundation of motherhood – of divinity – is already ingrained in me.

Recovery was all-consuming. I spent ample time at my doctor's; I still remember seeing my neurologist for the first time and immediately asking if I could have more children. Motherhood was my driving force. I suffered from PTSD and anxiety while navigating life as a survivor of a traumatic brain injury. My brain constantly played tricks on me. I often felt guilty for not being the mom that Mia deserves, and I constantly lived in fear she will be taken from me. In reality, I am still a hands-on parent, soon again volunteering in her classroom and attending all dance classes. But I still pushed my mind, body, and spirit to surpass all set boundaries.

I drove a car within three months. I passed all ongoing medical appointments and tests.

I traveled internationally. Two years into my recovery, I began to work. Collaborative work within the industries I have been most passionate about was complete synergy. Although I was uncertain whether I could successfully advance at work, the process pushed my brain more than anyone thought possible. I went from being a part-time writer for Tony Robbins Mastermind, to managing a publicity department for a national firm, to launching my Public Relations Firm. This uncharted path I navigated finally gave me back my confidence and security in motherhood. I was no longer afraid.

The Covid Pandemic demanded stillness, which proved to be an asset in my development. Even Anthony's struggle with covid exposes a new vigor. He faced underlying conditions stemming from his time as a World Trade Center First Responder. However, the unusual placidity allowed him a realignment of mind, body, and spirit. Simultaneously, his fertility magically improved.

When learning this, I quickly scheduled a tubal flush to ensure no blockage of my fallopian tubes. Two weeks later we were expecting.

I am writing this as I am 37 weeks pregnant with our son, Valentino Jovanni. Through my journey, I have come face-to-face with divinity. Motherhood has spoken to me in many ways on various occasions. It still leads back to Mother Mary, a human who became divine through her journey of motherhood.

My baby is a divine blessing, a miracle that will strengthen me, and my family, even more.

~ Divinity Speaking ~

"Divinity speaks differently to all. However, I have learned that divinity can be felt in the darkest of moments when your heart is lit with pure silence."

ABOUT THE AUTHOR
AMANDA RUMORE

Amanda Rumore is a Published Author, Speaker & Founder of The Publicity Collective. She uses her profound experiences in perseverance, spirituality as well as health and wellness to better cultivate her world.

As a wife and mom, she beat incredible odds and survived a harrowing Traumatic Brain Injury. After plummeting 40-feet from an Energy Vortex in the Red Rocks of Sedona, AZ, Amanda learned that energy is the foundation of life, and it can beautifully coincide with religions around the globe.

Originally from Chicago, IL., she studied at Arizona State University. Amanda then moved to Los Angeles and worked as a Hollywood Publicist. She has since worked throughout the U.S. in entrepreneurship, public relations and media roles before settling back into the Phoenix-area.

Amanda is determined to share her journey with the world.

Website: www.amandarumore.com

Website: www.thepublicitycollective.com

4

THE TRUTH WE KNOW

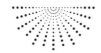

ANDREA BLINDT

*H*eat pulsed through my body as the doctor's words filled my ears.

"...there is no cure, the only treatment is supportive care to manage symptoms... no quality of life... admit to the hospital to fade away...". My son was almost three, and his life consisted of constant nausea, projectile vomiting, and constant pain that could not be eased. It was heartbreaking not having solutions or the ability to comfort him, so when we were approved for diagnostic work up after three years of fierce advocacy we clung to hope.

We trusted that if we knew the devil we were dealing with, we could battle it more wisely. Our doctors were stumped and without further insight we were limited in the progress we could make. That morning, as we went into the hospital, we prayed for answers. We believed we could overcome anything if we knew what was ahead. But when the doctor explained our son's diagnosis, and poor prognosis, I froze as fear crept back into my mind.

I imagined life without my beautiful son in it. I envisioned surviving the death of another child, the tiny wooden box of ashes that held my first twins' remains seared into my memory. Panic, sadness, and anger consumed me, and I thought I might collapse onto the hospital floor. "This can't be my life," I thought, as the doctor's words and abrasive alarms stole my hope. My chest squeezed as I inhaled willing air into my lungs, as though I was trying to suck cement through a coffee straw. My eyes fixed on the doctor's mouth as it moved, his words desolate, defeating, and limiting. Until suddenly I couldn't hear a thing and my eyes glossed over.

As the room blurred, I felt my body as it moved backwards away from this reality. I blinked, clearing my vision, and in that moment, clarity set in. Peace washed over me, extinguishing the fire I felt burning in my soul, and my body calmed. Air made its way easily into my lungs and my heart pumped a deep knowing through my body. A tiny whisper moved through my mind assuring me that it would be ok, and I clung to that belief. I didn't have the answers, or even know if a cure was possible, but I knew that everything I had learned as a nurse through my medical training and life experiences had led me to this very moment, and I had the ability to lean in and utilize it all.

I decided at that moment that I wasn't going to let the doctor, or this diagnosis define what my son's future would look like. Instead, I vowed to find a way to help my son, and I knew if I couldn't find the way, I would create one. I was determined as I gathered our belongings and left the hospital. The doctor told me there would be a team meeting in two weeks to discuss the plan of care moving forward. That meant I had two weeks to create a game plan. A million thoughts flew through my mind as I drove home. I knew that in order to heal our son, radical changes needed to happen, and I would need my husband's full support in order to successfully pull it off. I walked into the house and calmly sat at the counter across from my husband. He patiently listened to me as I detailed the day's events and test results. His face fell and his shoulders slumped forward as I spoke, heavy grief moving through him. I shifted in my seat feeling deep within my soul our ability to heal our son. I told my husband my plan and he rose from his chair, moved towards me, and wrapped me in a strong hug. Warm tears saturated my hair as he wept, tears of sorrow, hope, and gratitude. He cupped my face in his hands and told me he believed in me and knew that I would find a way to help our son. The amount of confidence his belief built in me, and my deep love for our son, pushed me forward in search of solutions.

I researched our son's disorder, looked for survivors, and sat in silence as wisdom and insight poured through me. I decided that everything needed to change. We would no longer be caring for our son the way we had been instructed to for three years. Instead, I would listen to my inner knowing and honor him as an individual. I stopped doing what doctors told me to do and started doing what I knew to be right. I stopped force feeding him the crappy diet that was laced in chemicals and additives and started increasing his intake of clean foods that were easy to digest and were supportive to his body. I stopped administering medications that were supposed to help his symptoms but caused multiple side effects while providing no relief. I stopped allowing the doctors' prognosis and limiting beliefs to be heard in our home. I stopped talking about his challenges, and instead I spoke life and truth into existence. I created a recording for him to listen to that affirmed his ability to heal and he listened to it multiple times a day. His body started to heal. He went from vomiting 12 times a day to 11 times, and with each small step in the right direction, we praised him and his body for its ability to thrive.

I sought additional support from multiple alternative medical practitioners and as our son continued to improve, we praised our combined efforts. The momentum was contagious, and we knew we were making strides. During our team meeting the head doctor applauded our achievements and told me that she supported me on this journey. I was told that most of the children who are diagnosed with this disorder are in the hospital, but since I was doing a great job of managing his care at home that I could continue to do so. They let me know that they would be available to discuss symptom management and quality of life with me when this treatment stopped working. I dismissed the possibility of my efforts not being successful and held onto the beliefs I had. As I affirmed them, it propelled me even further.

After a few months of our son seeing various specialists 3-4 times a week, my husband encouraged me to go back to school in order to deepen my knowledge and ability to practice the ancient wisdom our current practitioners were utilizing to help us support our son.

I was nervous. The idea felt big, out of my reach, a bit woo woo, and would cost a lot of time, resources, and finances. Our son's medical providers were all out of pocket and the organic food and supplement program we had him on cost us about $1,200 a week. We were already struggling to make ends meet after my husband lost his job due to needing to care for our other three children while I was researching, going to medical appointments, and caring for our son; and I couldn't imagine taking on another expense. My husband assured me in his ability to support me and our home while I committed to learning. I again sat in silence as I listened for confirmation on what direction to go. I, of course, had a million reasons not to do it, but as doors began to open and opportunities became available to me, I embraced the divine timing of it all and enrolled in multiple programs. Within a matter of weeks, I had enough confidence to begin treating our son on my own. I was absorbing the material quickly and it felt known to me, like a hidden treasure tucked deep within my soul eagerly waiting to be uncovered. My son continued to improve, his pain decreased, and his episodes of vomiting became less frequent. Our family was starting to heal and that brought me fulfillment and peace.

It took me close to three years to complete all of my training. I became certified in homeopathy, flower essences, Rapid

Transformational Therapy, Hypnotherapy, Neurolinguistic Programing, Emotional Freedom Technique, Life Coaching, Applied Kinesiology, and multiple other healing modalities. The additional wisdom I gained has not only changed my son's life, it also changed my life, my family's, and now hundreds of patients all around the world whom I have the privilege of sharing it with.

I am grateful for my husband, children, family, and teachers who supported me in honoring my inner knowing. Their support and guidance are invaluable, and with them I was able to create a life bigger than I ever imagined. Today, instead of relying on others for the answers, wisdom, and medical care I need, I search within. I utilize my personal healing journey along with my diverse medical training, to reassemble the broken parts of our medical system and fully strengthen the body, mind, and soul. I empower my patients to do the same, and I teach them how to unearth the wisdom they have within in order to create lives they love.

Through all of this I have learned that divine wisdom can be found in many places, shapes, and forms. It is available to us all and when we learn to listen to it, we are limitless.

~ Divinity Speaking ~

"My desire is for you to know that you are capable of creating a life you love. And that regardless of your diagnosis or prognosis, hope is still available. You don't need to enroll in a course, or spend a fortune seeing specialists, the answers exist in and around you. All you need to do is sit in silence and listen to the wisdom within. Once you receive the answers, I encourage you to bravely take the next step."

ABOUT THE AUTHOR

ANDREA BLINDT

Andrea Blindt is a registered nurse, holistic health practitioner, four-time international best-selling author, inspirational speaker, and life and mindset coach who empowers others through her own personal healing journey. She makes healing an inside job and guides her clients as they discover ways to strengthen their body, mind, and heart. This allows them to reclaim their power, advocate for what is in their best interest, and learn the tools needed to make decisions that are in alignment with their beliefs. Andrea believes that when people are informed, supported, and empowered they are better equipped to make health decisions. She has been featured in Authority's Medium Magazine, Bustle, Shefinds, Mel, Natural Health Radio, and multiple other publications and podcasts. She lives in California with her husband and four beautiful children. She loves being in nature, reading, writing, and inspiring others to create a life they love.

Website: www.andreablindt.com

Instagram: www.instagram.com/andreablindt

Email: heal@andreablindt.com

5
FOLLOWING THE GOLDEN THREAD

ANNELISA VALLERY

For me, Divinity means Spirit. It is the Cosmic Intelligence that unites us all. It is the Golden Thread that runs through all of Life, seen and unseen. I am grateful for the Golden Thread of my life.

My dad came to visit and spend time with my younger sister, Alix, and I in the city we lived in at the time, Philadelphia, Pennsylvania. It would be the first time in 10+ years he came to see us in the city where we lived, and I was excited. He had a blast just being with us and watching us fuss about which adventure we were going to take him on each day and how to get there. The pilot and the co-pilot he called us. He was quite amused and entertained.

One day, after dropping Alix off to work, we decided to walk down to the end of South Street. There is a little park on one side and a bridge that takes you to a vista point where you can look past the zooming cars on the highway below and out onto the water where the restaurant boats are docked. Many people hang out in this area and in the summer, many people sell an assortment of goods including bottles of water.

We walked over the bridge to the vista point, where we stood and chatted for a moment. Then we walked back over the bridge towards the car. A little girl and her father were sitting on the right side of the brick sidewalk. The father was sitting on a big cooler. He offered us a cold bottle of water and we declined. We continued to walk and talk, and then the little girl, no more than four, walked up to me and offered a cold bottle of water. I asked her how much and she said $1. I responded: "I am so sorry darling; I don't have a dollar on me." She responded "Okay" and walked away. I walked away totally taken by how adorable she was and disappointed that I didn't have $1. Dad and I were waiting to cross the street when he said, "You really love kids. It really hurt your heart to tell her no."

I was caught off guard by his comment as it was the first time in years Dad had seen me around children. So my inner rebellious teenager was fussing, "Who are you? You don't know me." Even though he is my father, I wanted him to be wrong. Yet, still his observation was spot on.

I have always loved working with children and yet when preparing to go to college, it was so clear to me that it would not be the field that I served in. In high school, friends, teachers, and coaches thought I'd be a pediatric doctor or nurse, somewhere working with kids and in health. I knew that I loved health, wellness, home remedies (aka homeopathy or naturopathy) and I loved children but serving in a place that included both, absolutely not. All I could see was me working with kids in healthcare and being an emotional wreck. All I saw was me in somebody's psychiatric ward, on someone's therapy couch, shriveled into a ball because I didn't know how to distinguish or navigate my emotions while serving in that space. At that time, most of my days were spent avoiding my emotions. So doing my heart's work outside of my body was absolutely NOT a happening thing. So I dug my heels into healthcare and stayed for a while.

Fast forward to my mid-twenties. I was now working in clinical research, dating a guy also in healthcare, whose son was in college at the time. He marveled at the way I could be with kids - totally at peace. We were out at a family event where there were several children around playing. We were sitting next to one another on chairs and at some point, I was called to the floor to be with and play with the children. I sat there in the middle of all the children playing, screaming, laughing, and talking. I was totally relaxed and observing the children play, being with all that was happening around me. He says, "That. Right there" pointing at me. "You are so at peace in the middle of all of that chaos." Later that afternoon as we headed home, he shared, "I don't understand. You were so at peace in the middle of the children running around, screaming, playing, banging... You were so unbothered by it." He was completely baffled and that has always stayed with me. It was funny to me because I thought nothing of it.

I had forgotten that as a pre-teen, I helped run the church daycare. This is the place where all the parents dropped their kids off so they can go to enjoy service in peace. We had babies, toddlers through to about seven-year-olds.

A fellow congregant who would drop off her three boys to the church daycare, noticed how good I was with her boys and offered me a baby-sitting job. The boys were about 1-2 years apart and quite rambunctious. When she and her husband would go to events, I would babysit the boys in their beautiful Victorian home. We had so much fun playing freeze tag, races, and anything I created on the fly to keep them engaged and in one room. For me, the name of the game was to keep them in one room which proved to be a challenge at times. Then my family moved from North Carolina to Pennsylvania. Funnily enough, our neighbor, behind us, had three boys also. Alex, Derek, and Jared, all two years apart, similar ages to the three boys I babysat for in North Carolina. We had a blast!

Fast forward to my late twenties, two friends and I were creating an organization that supported those moving through homelessness to have a life where all their basic needs were met. As I did research on our target group, I discovered the correlations between foster care and teen/youth homelessness. I was shocked and dumbfounded. This sparked a desire to serve teens and youth, yet I could tell I was still too close to the woman I saw as a teenager on someone's therapy couch. I still had more inner healing work to do. Then I moved from Pennsylvania to California because it was time for a change. This change I called Divine Intervention.

After I first arrived in California, I met a friend who has been a longtime LA county social worker, mental health advocate and therapist. I shared with her my desire to work with teens and youth, and she recommended I become a CASA (Court Appointed Special Advocate) for LA County. I was so excited that I was finally able to fulfill this pull on my heart. When I got home that night, I researched CASA, and reviewed the application. The application was several pages long with open ended questions about my experience and what I have to contribute to foster children and their families. It was the last question that was confronting for me. Then I looked at the last question and my inner response was, "Whew, I don't know about this." I knew I wasn't ready yet, but I was closer. I was closer to being grounded and centered in my authentic being and could see my past experiences from a higher vantage point, but I wasn't there yet. It took me 2-3 additional years of inner healing work to be at a place where I was confident in my ability to be an advocate for teens/youth and to be with whatever they brought. In 2017, I was sworn in as a CASA and spent 4.5 years volunteering as a CASA before founding my own non-profit, Causing Legacy Inc., to serve black and brown teens and youth in a larger capacity.

Meanwhile, I met a sister friend who discovered she was pregnant with her sixth child. Although she initially inquired if I knew about any black doulas or midwives, one night as we were discussing her pregnancy journey, our conversation began to shift from her pregnancy to me considering being a doula. I was uncertain as that was not a world, I considered stepping into before, so it felt somewhat foreign. I had a moment, call it a gut feeling, that made me nervous. Intuitively, I heard, I am to guide and support her on this journey. So, I asked her the question that intuitively bubbled up for me to ask: "Am I your doula?" She answered with a resounding, "YES!"

My thoughts began to race, my body started sweating as the nervous feeling expanded and my stomach was even more unsettled. I had very little clue about labor, delivery, let alone birthing a whole human being in the world. As she started to share more of her racing thoughts, I asked that she pause. I took a moment to pause myself, took a deep breath and I allowed the racing thoughts to quiet down. First, I closed my eyes, focused inwardly, and I surrendered. I let go of all the 'I don't know' and 'how am I going to do this" thoughts. I accepted Spirit will guide me along the way and then I responded to my friend: "Yes."

The moment I said yes, the racing thoughts disappeared, my body stopped sweating and this sense of peace and calm came over me. As my friend shared her delight and assured me she would have another (more experienced) doula support her with prenatal, labor and delivery. We both marveled at the beautiful moment that unfolded between us. Although she had birthed her other children in a hospital setting, she was being called to birth this child differently. It was her first water birth, no meds, no hospital, no doctors, simply trusting her body, her team (partner, doulas, midwife, and support team) and Spirit. This was my introduction to being a birth worker.

Fast forward to 2022, having a casual conversation with another sister friend who shared that she would have me as her doula if she chose to have more children. When I shared my initial thoughts of uncertainty, she replied with a beautiful message from Spirit delivered with tears of conviction affirming the contribution that I am and what I get to bring to the birthing realm. I was a little surprised and my inner response was, "Alright Spirit, I got the message and I will follow the breadcrumbs." This was a Saturday.

Later that day, I emailed a doula I had followed for a couple years and appreciated the diversity and integrated knowledge she shares about the birth world. Out of curiosity, I inquired as to when her next doula training class was scheduled for. She responded, we start Tuesday and there is still space to join. I joined the class on Monday, and I have experienced so many moments of, "Now I see Spirit, now I understand."

In my first doula class, as my teacher was sharing about all that being a birth worker encompasses, I realized all the lived experiences I had moved through, lessons learned and integrated, and my continued self-development are wrapped up in this role as a mastery application. Now that I unpacked the impactful events of my life and I have equipped myself with the tools, energy healing modalities and knowledge to navigate my emotions while continuing to dive deeper, I want to serve in my heart space where I can apply both my knowledge and my heart to really make a difference in the world. There is a fulfillment that I had not yet experienced that now feels like it is present and forthcoming.

My life now is an answer to a prayer that I didn't know that I made as a teenager. I now have the knowledge, the tools, the awareness and the skillset to support myself and others in navigating all that we move through as we birth new life into this world and rebirth ourselves. I am beyond grateful for all the families I get to support in bringing new life into this world.

~ *Divinity Speaking* ~

"Pay attention. Pay attention to the messages, songs, conversations, places, or things that resonate deeply in your heart. They are guiding you. Listen, listen always, and listen deeply. Listen for the whispers of Spirit. Spirit is always guiding you."

ABOUT THE AUTHOR

ANNELISA VALLERY

AnneLisa Vallery is a teens/youth advocate, keynote speaker, holistic wellness coach, doula and the founder and President of Causing Legacy. Through her service as a CASA (Court Appointed Special Advocate) for children and teens in the Los Angeles County foster care system, her relationships with her elders and her own healing journey, AnneLisa was inspired to serve BIPOC teens and youth on a larger scale and be a bridge for intergenerational connections. Through Causing Legacy, she facilitates experiences that honor the elders' wisdom and contribute to teens and youth by providing them with the tools and resources to heal, guidance to navigate the inner journey and support to discover who they are in the world. AnneLisa has been featured in the Turning Season Podcast where she shares how Causing Legacy is part of the "turning season".

Website: www.causinglegacy.org

Instagram: @annelisavallery; @causinglegacy

Facebook: @causinglegacy

Email: annelisa@causinglegacy.org

6

SURRENDER TO THE MAGIC
OF LOVE

ASHLEY ABRAMSON

I was unworthy of love. My truest self to be exact was the one unworthy – or so I thought! My soul always knew it was worthy of love. It was the external environment that showed me that my truest self was unworthy of love. I assumed this through the reactions and actions from those around me.

My grandfather left because I wasn't good enough. My stepfather left because I was too difficult. My father left because life was too difficult. And then my husband left because I wasn't enough – or so I thought. These were the narratives driving my actions, reactions and outlook on life for decades. All of the males in my life left me, and in turn I internalized this belief that it was because of me and that I was unworthy of love from *any* male.

I tried my hardest to prove my worth by setting aside my own values and feelings to please the men in my life, hoping they'd stick around. I was a chameleon constantly changing to what I thought I needed to present as in order to be worthy of love. I did my best every time to be exactly what I thought they needed me to be so that they didn't leave. And it never worked: they always left.

Love for me was always perceived as something external. To be loved or to have love was an action gained only by external forces. Falling in love was the ultimate goal, the way that Hollywood had portrayed in the movies I watched growing up. It was a magical fairytale that as a child felt so real and obtainable. As I grew up society taught me that in fact that was false, that is not love but rather a fairy tale that was fake and far from the true reality we lived in.

Instead love meant sacrifice, struggle, and settling for comfort. Love meant being someone that you felt could be loveable, not the person you are at the core. You were only loveable if you became the person that the adults around you and society told you to be. Love was not just a birth right but instead a constant job of external actions to obtain.

In my mind loving yourself was a selfish action. Taking care of yourself and putting yourself first was not something that was seen as loveable in my world. Someone who sacrificed themselves for others and did what others expected them to do was the definition of a loveable person for me. So again love was always something external, something you gave to others or received from others, never something you gave or received from yourself. It was a chore, a full time job that you never received the exact training for.

I was able to survive like this for years, maintaining a sense of love from the external, though never genuinely happy in any area of my life or about myself. Constantly fulfilling the duties of this job that was bestowed upon me at birth that I had no clue how to do. I would set goals on my body image and when I hit them it was never enough. I would complete a project at work and again it was never good enough, so I would seek validation from the external world to grade the outcome. I was constantly seeking love and acceptance from others in order to feel worthy.

I anchored the majority of this need in the men that were in my life at that time. My father left me at eighteen and he was the last nonintimate male figure I sought out love from, so I turned to my ex-boyfriend at the time (who eventually became my husband) to fulfill that role. He did provide this, as well as my son that I had adopted. But it was bound to crumble one day because the foundation it was built on was non-existent. And it did, the last male I believed would show me unconditional love had found someone new to love and he was leaving me. This reinforced the strong narrative I had been living most of my life and it solidified that I truly was unworthy of love.

My world was flipped-turned upside down and not the good kind like The Fresh Prince of Bel-Air. I remember thinking to myself that I had no man left to love me. I must be so unworthy of love. So subconsciously I set out on a mission to prove this to myself and the world. Indeed I did through my actions, though at the same time I was seeking any and all forms of love that I could find and many times it was the feeling of love received through one night stands, only to wake up the next morning feeling more unworthy than I had the day prior.

This path I was on was a very dark and destructive path and I came to the realization that I had two options: either continue down this path or learn how to heal myself. I chose to do the work of healing myself. I was blessed with many guides on this journey that provided me with support and a space that was free from judgment to explore and find my way back home to my most authentic self. For me this journey meant finding out who the heck I really was because for so long I was a chameleon and tried to be everything that I thought others wanted me to be.

Along this journey of healing myself, I was faced with uncovering the narratives I had been living by and one of the strongest was that I was unworthy of love from anyone else and most of all from myself. This narrative had started when I was very young, when I would be loud and bold. Instead of receiving love I would receive anger and frustration from those most important to me. Not because they were doing this to hurt me but because my energy was intense and at times uncomfortable for others.. I remember when I would get so excited and filled with love that I would be so full of energy I didn't know what to do with it. So I would be loud and do outrageous things. I was immediately told to stop and not do that. This stored in my subconscious that the feelings I was having were not valid and worthy of expression, that the love and excitement I felt was not correct.

Again overtime I began to lock that part of me away and instead be the person that was worthy of love, according to the constructs of society and those around me. This caused me to become someone I was not at all. I started to resent myself and those around me, turning me into a person filled with frustration, confusion and anger. I had locked away my truest self due to the others around me.

I made it my mission to become the Ashley that I once was. The one so pure and filled with love, the one who loved herself and everything about life. Because the state of my life and current reality I was living was miserable and inauthentic, I looked for the child hidden inside of me.

My spiritual mentor, who was male, was the final piece to my healing journey. I fell in love with him, or so I thought. He told me at the beginning that he would never go anywhere and that he would always be there for me which was not something I had ever experienced. I felt a love so immense that I had never felt in a relationship with a male before. I was seen and accepted as I truly was. He provided a space free of judgment where I could truly be myself and he didn't leave. I viewed this as a love from him because that is how I had sought out love for decades prior. This journey though was not created for finding love externally but instead finding unconditional love for myself. Once our journey was over and I reflected on this love, I realized I did not fall in love with him, in fact I had fallen in love with myself through the reflection he provided for me.

He was only reflecting back the immense love and acceptance I had finally obtained for myself. He was only able to do this because I had found my way back home to myself fully. He would not have been able to reflect this if in fact I did not feel it about myself.

This realization was immense. It was the first time I was able to own that love within, instead of placing it on an external person or action. This brought a huge awareness in my growth journey that the 'job' I felt had been bestowed upon me at childhood, that I had no clue how to do, was actually within me all along. It was so easy that at times I questioned its validity. All I had to do was be myself and love all of myself, take care of myself and in turn life just started to fall into place. I no longer felt a need to find love because, well I had love, so instead I began showing love to all around me.

As time passed I started to get an inner yearning for that soul in human form to do life with. I immediately started questioning myself, where was I not loving myself that now I am needing external love again?! I remember asking a friend this. She assured me that in fact this was not a need but instead a longing because my soul had done the work it needed in order to unite with the soul here on earth that I would complete the rest of my days here with. When she said this, it felt so right, like a weight had been lifted off me with the realization that I did not need to search. Only when I fully surrender in life is when the path is fully revealed to me. I had found this on my personal growth journey; truly being open to the universe and listening to that call inside that I call 'a soul dance party' and surrendering to whatever unfolds. In the past I have found that when I try to initiate I am pushing against the universe, letting my imagination (which is limited to prior experience) create what reality looks like.

I revisited a list I had written in my journal regarding the soul mate I was wanting to attract, that I had written some months earlier. I was astounded to realize how ego driven this list was. There were thirty-plus detailed qualities I was looking for in a soul mate but many had to do with looks, financial status etc. I realized that this list no longer aligned with my way of thinking and that the ego driven attributes were no longer necessary.

As time passed I noticed that I was constantly evaluating all of the male relationships in my life with "were they the one?" only to come to the realization that again I was searching instead of just allowing the journey to unfold. On February 11th 2022 I again wrote down in my journal what I was looking for in a soulmate, though this time my intention was to write from my soul and fully surrender to the journey. I created a list that was only fourteen long. I did not have any expectation from this list other than letting the universe know that I was ready.

Shortly after I wrote this list I went to lunch with a friend. We had been scheduled to have lunch months prior but it didn't end up working out. Randomly we reconnected and rescheduled . At lunch she asked if I was dating. I shared with her that I wasn't, but that recently I felt like I was ready for that person to show up. She asked what I was doing to find this person, my response was "they will come along". She immediately challenged that statement and proceeded to invite me into a challenge to give online dating a try for thirty days. I was never one to be interested in the use of online applications for dating and the only time I had tried them was right after my divorce to once again receive external gratification through matching and chatting.

But when she challenged me to this, I felt a pull inside of me to accept the challenge. I went home, thought about it and within a few days created my profile. I had no expectations from this and actually gave this venture very limited time from me. At this time in my journey I had realized the value of my time and energy and I did not want to spend too much of this important commodity, so I allocated ten minutes a day and my first question immediately got to business. I asked what the most recent podcast or book was that they had consumed. I figured that I wanted someone who craved growth and awakening as much as myself and knowing what information they are consuming could tell me a lot immediately.

I had thousands of interests on my account immediately and I was very overwhelmed. Most matches either were not consuming any knowledge currently or just didn't feel a fit.

Then on day three which was exactly one month after I had written the person I was wanting to attract in my journal, I matched with a man that had a smile that intrigued me. He also, interestingly enough, had a cover photo of himself with a snowman and though I had moved to Florida I was a Minnesota girl at heart and I loved building snowmen.

He responded to my question, answering that he had read the book *Flow*. This again intrigued me as it's a book that is sought out by a person that has a certain understanding of this universe and our part in it. So the conversation continued and eventually we met for coffee. This date was meant to only last an hour but two hours flew by and although it was not filled with constant conversation, the pauses were not awkward. There was something there, a knowingness that I had never felt before.

I immediately told my best friend that I was going to stop pursuing anyone else and focus my energy on this guy. A week later we went on another date and I wrote in my journal that he was the one, but I still questioned it as recently I had evaluated all relationships looking for the one. I asked myself was this me again forgetting to follow the journey and create something that wasn't really there? I noted that thought and continued riding this knowingness I had inside.

The way he looked at me was a way I had never felt before, it sparked great curiosity in me and also an awareness that he was a mirror of what I felt about myself as well. Before our third date he texted that he was sick. My friend called that a red flag, that he was no longer interested, but I felt differently and didn't jump on that bandwagon. I trusted my gut.

Then Sunday morning he called and asked if I was going to the beach that day. I said yes I was (I went every Sunday which he knew) and then immediately regret started to creep in. Sundays at the beach were *my* days to refuel. I did things like painting, making sand castles and just fully fueling my inner child and soul. All things that I had been taught were not loveable and embarrassing. I had three options. 1) I pretend to be someone I am not and conform to what a beach day 'should' look like according to society. 2) I uninvite him. 3) I honor the person I am, giving him the heads up and he can take it or leave it.

I went over this in my head anxiously. I really liked this guy and though I had learned to love myself I still had not been this person around someone I was intimately interested in. So I sent him a message informing him that Sundays at the beach were for me to refuel. I did not get all dolled up and I typically painted, built sand castles or anything my inner child requested. It may not be entertaining to him but that he was welcome to come. When I hit send I thought for sure that would seal the deal but it didn't. He responded stating that he sketches sometimes and would bring his stuff to do so.

That day at the beach is when I knew that the movies I had watched growing up were in fact reality. Fairy Tales do exist. I never knew I could love another soul as much as I do, nor did I believe that love was truly meant to grow stronger every day instead of fading overtime. It does though. Every day my love grows stronger and the things that would irritate me are what makes him unique and I love him even more for that.

I was never able to receive a love like this because I was never able to love myself like this. Only by learning to unconditionally love myself am I able to love another soul this way and to receive a love like this from another. I could only attract my soulmate by first healing myself and surrendering to the path in which I made it there.

We are taught that love is meant to be work and that in order to have it we must settle and deal with dislikes from the other. I have found that this is in fact false. The soul we are meant to spend the rest of our life with will feel right, you will be faced with many signs, synchronicities and an overwhelming sense of knowingness. With everyday and every new irritation your love will only grow stronger and it starts the minute you begin by starting the small actions of loving yourself. Go buy yourself the flowers and tell yourself every morning in the mirror that you love you and all of you. When you begin to love yourself and truly surrender to the universe others around you will begin to love you for it.

~ Divinity Speaking ~
"Learning to love yourself unlocks the magic of receiving love from others and the universe."

ABOUT THE AUTHOR

ASHLEY ABRAMSON

Ashley is a Mentor for Divorced Women. She mentors the raw woman after divorce to discover newfound confidence and joy by rebuilding her purpose-filled life from the ground up.

After a 15 year relationship, Ashley found her life flipped upside down through divorce. She was hopeless, broken, lost and alone. The focus of her profession at the time was healing the inner children of her clients. That's when she realized she needed to heal her own inner child.

Her goal is to blend her wisdom and expertise on the impact of childhood trauma and her own experience to rebuild and heal after divorce. She uses a strengths-based approach to help women find their magically authentic selves after divorce.

Ashley believes that you are Divorced, not Destroyed and that every woman deserves to live her most magical life . Her podcast, The Unicorn Effect, provides the support for whatever sh*t is pulling you down that day. Ashley is also an international best-selling author.

Website: www.coachwithashley.net

Instagram: @ash_abramson

7

THE ART AND SCIENCE OF DIVINE INCARNATION

BRANDY KNIGHT

*E*veryday I show up to my life, to my work, to my mission with the openness to receive the Divine information that is being transmitted to me by the other parts of me and my team from the higher realms. This level of receptivity is crucial for the awakening work I am doing during this life. For myself and others.

More recently I have been going deeper with the concepts and experiences of incarnation which has been truly invaluable in regards to adding clarity to how I show up in guiding others through the process of stepping out of the matrix during this time and space. Contributing to these awakening processes is my destiny in this life. I am the sacred Lioness who embodies profound peace and tranquility by connecting to the protective power of this sword. I am Shanti Teg Kaur.

Incarnation is a term that most people are familiar with, yet some have not quite understood the magnitude of specific detail that goes into incarnation.

From what I know to be true, we incarnate into a physical life experience to learn from contrast. This contrast can be as simple as, last life I was short and this life I am tall, to last life I was an abuser and this life I was sexually abused. It is the contrast that we learn and grow the most from as souls.

I don't spend too much time pondering my previous lives because remaining in the here and now is of the utmost importance to my work here, however, I do find this concept of the contrast created from other lives extremely helpful in navigating some harsh timelines during this life. I show up as a spiritual alchemist during this life. Available to me are the natural elements, the way of the ether, plant and root communications from underground and above, celestial communications, and sound and light codes from the highest realms.

In my human body, I can act as a translator so others can understand the subtle messages available to them. This ability is vital when it comes to propelling humankind and the great mother essence into the golden age. We are in the thick of the great awakening at this moment. Being able to guide and hold space for others as they integrate their awakening into their lives is my mission.

Instead of telling about how I use divinity in my life, I'd like to show you an example of how I utilize it daily through divinely received transmission. The majority of information that has been coming through has to do with the state of things on this planet and how it potentially affects a soul's journey. This information is quite intense and in truth as I write this I am still processing and organizing the information that has been coming through as I upgrade my nervous system in order to sustain the gravity of this information.

The following is a message from my team which consists of earth me, soul me, my teachers, my Deva guides, the elementals, and my soul family. You'll notice a shift between the use of the words "we" and "you" which indicates what frequency is coming forward with that particular piece of information. For example, earth me, soul me, my teacher, and my soul family will use "we" indicating that we are all in this together. The Deva guides and elementals will use "you" as they often take the supportive observer role. "We" is also used when the team comes through all together at once. While I was writing, the information was coming through so fast that it was challenging to keep up. I found this process to be an amazing opportunity to stretch my gifts beyond what they previously were.

It is important to mention that by reading further you agree to take full responsibility for your experience as a new/deeper activation of truth that applies specifically to your destiny will be taking place. The words here are for you to metabolize in your unique way. The shift might be subtle or massive.

Please keep in mind that the Divine message from my team might be different from the Divine message from yours, and they are all massively important.

If this does not feel like a yes for you, I strongly encourage you to move on to the next chapter and revisit it here when you are ready.

If this does feel like a yes for you well then...I'll see you on the other side!

"Hello, dear soul spirits. We come here to connect with you on this lush planet as thought-form frequency. We are so happy you are reading this. We hope that the words on these pages add a greater level of density and substance to our message here today. We truly appreciate your attention.

You have chosen human life.

Oh, what a rich experience the human planets offer. Such detail goes into choosing your human host, and you chose well! Such precision goes into holding that stream of light and sound, connecting and blending with the human fetus and you did it perfectly!

Earth is considered one of the most challenging planets to incarnate on. Human existence on planet Earth, as some call it, is both exquisite and torturous. The realms of heaven and hell are both available to us here on this planet. Can you sense that? Can you see how earth's natural elements are so wonderfully healing and beautiful and also brutal and barbaric? These two sides, the beautiful and the barbaric are always available for use in any given situation to focus on. How you are focused is the key ingredient for the success of your incarnation. Just by your focus, you can choose a hellish or heavenly existence.

At this moment we can feel that part of you can sense that this chapter is meant for you to read. As if we are being received or channeled here to put sound and light codes on this page specifically for you.

This sense is a knowing and your knowing is correct.

We have been called here today to support you as you continue to open up layer by layer, to what is actually at play here on this planet. It now goes beyond this planet and this life. You can sense this now. You can now begin to remember why you chose this life. The fog of amnesia is lifting. The glowing flame of your being knows now, that you are here to help liberate your fellow soul spirits from the haze that covers the planet.

We can sense that you are filled with such love. Let the flame of love and passion grow inside your heart and expand into and beyond your auric field.

We would now like to invite you at this moment to stretch your arms up to embrace the sky, take a long deep breath in and out and let your heart center expand.

Now let us speak more on incarnation into physical form.

To incarnate requires the highest levels of courage. When you are ready to take physical form again you are aware of the potential hardships and blessings awaiting you. This is not always an easy decision on the part of the soul spirit. However, choosing to incarnate offers us soul spirits a potential fast track in soul evolution in comparison to choosing to not incarnate and remain at home base to learn the lessons necessary to evolve.

Physical life is chosen for vast many reasons. Not all of those reasons are a repercussion related to what is considered karma. Yet all of these reasons contain the intention to learn and grow. Often a previous life will look like the complete opposite of your current incarnation. This can indicate a more advanced soul who thrives with extreme contrast for maximum progress in making their accent. Other times a soul can be completely on the back burner while the human mind takes over completely in a hamster-wheel existence potentially indicating a less experienced soul. Some lifetimes can be very quick as to dip into a brief Karmic brush-up. Other lifetimes are long and exquisite. Whichever the lifetime details, you choose it all.

We understand that due to the amnesia put in place at the time you entered your physical host this might be challenging to accept. This concept of choosing it all. If you are reading this, you chose a life of many wonderful challenges. The lessons learned from the challenges are exactly why you are here now. The sole reason you choose to incarnate is to contribute to your soul's reason.

Before we go further it feels like a good time for you to ask yourself a few questions.

Have you remained on the path of your Destiny?

Have you been aware of the signs you agreed to receive that illuminate the path of destiny for you?

For example, reading this chapter is one of those signs. Can you sense that now?

Even if you do not have the answers to those questions at this moment, we can feel that you are beginning to experience that the response of "I don't know" is merely the subconscious mind participating in avoidance behavior. We can sense the veil of amnesia getting thinner and your awakening taking place. Congratulations on your advancements.

Let us shift gears for a moment to the wondrous life in between incarnations. The space and place of the ultimate creative force from which we are all offshoots. Our home base we return to between every life regardless of physical form or planet of incarnation. Our family team supports one another honestly and lovingly through all stages of incarnation review. The home of our soul spirit in its entirety.

When you leave your physical planetary incarnation, you travel on a radiating beam of light and sound to come back to home base. This travel home can be so rejuvenating and soothing. Like every fiber of your essence being treated to an electrified massage. This is our path home. Once we arrive we are greeted by our teacher, guides, soul family members, and previous earth family members. There can sometimes be a grace period, for example, if a soul leaves a body quickly and/or tragically, where we might require extra support adjusting to being back home. Typically however this homecoming is exquisite. After our homecoming, it is time for review. Did you maximize your time in a host? What is the Karmic debt vs Karmic payoff? Things like this are reviewed in loving depth during your post-life review.

We can feel that part of you remembers this process.

We would like to get to our bigger point now. This is a complex conversation to have and a complex concept to grasp.

We at home base are very aware of what is taking place on the planet called earth. The more recent remarkable advances in technology both greatly support human life on planet earth and also greatly work against it. It is very possible that with certain advances on planet earth, the trip home between lives, as we travel on the beam of light and sound, for some, might be interrupted by these technologies.

Due to the plane of existence and the inhabitants of planet Earth entertaining the law of polarity, there can be an organic positive to every negative experience and vice versa. Including the circumstances that are unfolding on the planet currently. Typically this law of polarity provides a platform for creating somewhat of a what you could call a sacred balance. However, right now it is this so-called sacred balance that is being threatened in great ways. We can sense that you are very aware of this even if the words are not yet available for you to express it.

We would now like to lift another layer of the veil of amnesia away at this moment.

You see the age of technology has given way to wonderous advancements both celebratory and punishable. Some of the technologies that have been widely introduced more recently to humans on earth are geared toward separating the soul from the human host through a process that utilizes less dense matter such as artificial light, sound, vapor, and liquid materials. These technologies are being introduced and presented to humans on planet earth in a dishonest fashion. The information required to create the bases for informed consent in decision-making on an individual and community level is not being provided. Fear frequency has taken over in many moments on earth. Fear is being used to control humans. A fearful state is one of the easiest states in which a soul can go dormant in a human host, allowing the human mind to step off the path of destiny and into the hamster's wheel.

There are a large number of beings that have lost sight of their original mission for incarnation largely due to these technologies and tactics. They have allowed themselves to be hypnotized, overrun, and processed with low vibrational hypnotics that aim to redirect a soul's journey after the soul has left the physical host. It is of the highest importance that souls do not go dormant inside their host. It will take the great workings of the more advanced incarnated souls to shake the others out of their fear-induced slumber.

This current experience on planet earth is like no other. We are presented with something that goes beyond life and what some humans call death. There is quite possibly so much more at stake here than what is observable on the surface of the earth.

We can sense that you are becoming aware of the behind-the-scenes low vibrational agendas that have been manipulating lives and realities. We understand that these are very complex concepts. It is vital to continue your awakening and the sharpening of your awareness.

This awareness is something to celebrate!

You are something to celebrate!

Our job as team members from home base is to send you vital information. Sending information along the beam of light and sound that connects us to you is extremely advanced work. You can receive our information at any time if you are properly tuned in. However, due to amnesia, it is complex to send you information and even more complex for you to receive the transmissions we send. For humans on planet earth, your team is the clearest and loudest during the early morning hours of sunrise. Having an early morning spiritual practice is highly encouraged so you can receive your messages and recognize your signs. For example, the medium in which we are being called here through today is our earthly team member who has developed a very committed morning spiritual practice which aids in receiving and transmitting the information.

We at home base continually receive the information you transmit to us from the incarnations you are participating in at any given moment. We are here always to help you learn the lessons and create the change you intended to.   Change is created by physical incarnation. This is exactly why you choose to incarnate. To have the opportunity to progress as a soul and create change. That is the job of the soul spirit that has blended with a host. However, blending does not always stick. For example, a young soul might find a human mind overpowering, and end up fading into the background. When this occurs, there is often little growth and little change. However, all lives are celebrated because during after-life observation there is always an amount of valuable information to ponder and evaluate.

After leaving our physical host we make the journey home. The road to home base is one of light and sound as we mentioned previously. When we leave our physical hosts we return to our form of light and sound. As you know light and sound vibrate at a frequency that is less dense than physical form. Like riding a radiating liquid light vapor conveyer belt that can navigate the ethers with ease.

At this moment we would like to shift gears again and go over some aspects of the relationship between the human and the soul spirit.

From the moment your soul was created by the light of source frequency, you became infinite. We know that this is a complex concept. Once you were created as a soul spirit you became infinite. Always. Timeless. The measurement of time and chronology was created by physical beings to help make sense, observe and record change. In truth, there is no time. Only change. There is only an infinite collection of nows and within those collections of nows, there is change. Your physical forms during lifetimes will go through major change. As will your soul as it continues to evolve.

You as soul spirit chose this exact body, this exact life, this exact mission. You and your team went over every detail thoroughly. You all chose who played what role, where you would meet, and signs in which to recognize each other.

So now here are some questions.

What is your mission?

Why did you choose this life?

Can you start to identify your team members that have chosen to incarnate here with you?

Can you feel that you are a beacon of light for others?

If you are reading these words, you are a seeker of truth. A practitioner of the cosmic order. These words are here for you to propel you into a deeper understanding of what's at play and the vital role you chose to contribute to the salvation of physical life on planet earth and the souls that come to visit. Please know you are not ever alone in this. Call on your team, reach out to community, deepen your dedication, and expand your practice so you may experience all the support you have set up for yourself in this life.

It is time to be bold and courageous.

It is time to remember why you chose this life.

It is time to remember your divine destiny.

This feels like a good place to press pause on our transmission.

Thank you for your focus and attention.

You are truly appreciated and celebrated."

Greetings from the flip side!

Perhaps this information is completely new to you, or perhaps it is a loving reminder of what we are faced with here during this time and space. Our focus is crucial. It is up to us to lovingly shake awake those that are in a fear induced slumber. How you do this is your own unique recipe of lightworker. Of wayshower.

~ Divinity Speaking ~
"Let us disarm our enemies with the pure light of love so that the shell of their disguise falls away and their truth is revealed and healed."
So it is.

ABOUT THE AUTHOR

BRANDY KNIGHT

Brandy Knight, the Esoteric Exorcist, is an Emotional Health Specialist, Accountability Coach, Kundalini Yogic Scientist, International best selling and award winning author, and fierce alpha female mama bear. She has been featured in Authority Magazine, Thrive Global and Medium to name a few. Her mission in this life is to support those who have experienced trauma and or abuse and are not getting that "now my life has meaning and I am living my Destiny" experience from traditional psychotherapy and or psychiatry. Brandy tells her clients like it is with a dose of crass humor and endless love. Many that have worked with Brandy's Emotional Alchemy and Accountability Coaching have experienced incredible results in lightning fast speed. When not working she is out exploring nature with her lightworker daughter, snuggling her two spoiled kitties, and cracking crass ass jokes.

Website: www.innercaulling.com

Email: innercaulling@gmail.com

Instagram: www.instagram.com/innercaulling

Facebook: www.facebook.com/brandy.knight.39545

8

MESSAGES FROM THE PRAYING MANTIS

CAROL LOUISE SCHOFFMANN

Be still, go within, connect with your higher self
Listen to your inner voice, trust your instincts
Put aside your worries and fears
Have patience
Trust in divine timing

THE DIVINE IS ALWAYS SPEAKING

*S*pirituality Defined
Spirituality is a belief that we are part of a greater whole, and this meaningful connection is cosmic or divine in nature.

I have never been a religious person, but I became a spiritual one.

This chapter highlights my unexpected spiritual journey to healing energy work that began with Reiki training. Ultimately, Reiki and Meditation practices sharpened my keen intuition and expanded my spiritual intelligence. Serving others through this work, connects me to my divine nature and the divinity in everyone and everything.

We have all experienced pivotal moments in our lives that reinforce the belief that there is more to our reality than what meets the eye, or what occurs within the constraints of our logical mind. I certainly have experienced synchronicities, coincidences, miracles and magic. When I began trusting that none of these occurrences were random, I began tapping into the energy of the Universe.

The Divine is always speaking to me. It vibrates through energy and discovery, traveling in goosebumps, a knowing in my bones or whispers in the wind. Look around and listen, it's speaking to you too.

A REIKI AWAKENING

Opening Up To Spiritually Guided Energy

Reiki Defined

Reiki, (pronounced Ray-Key), means "spiritually guided universal life force energy" in Japanese. It is a gentle and effective healing art that balances the universal life force energy of the recipient, restoring health and well being.

In the Spring of 2015, I began to study Reiki again. While writing this, I remembered that I had taken a one day Reiki workshop sometime in the early 1990's, but I have almost no recollection of my initiation to it. I must not have been ready to embrace it then.

In the early 1990's, I held a Bachelor of Fine Arts and a Masters in Art Education. I was still creating and showing my own art. And I had opened a unique retail boutique, Badawang Art, which is still in existence. Twice a year, I traveled to the Far East, designing and importing art and craft for my boutique. I was immersed in an artistic community and explored holistic healing and spirituality. Then, my life path took many twists and turns over the next twenty five years, separating me from my art and the spiritual healing practices I had endeavored to explore back then.

In 2015, I was yearning to learn something new, that would help me look inwards, let go of worry, feel spacious and guide me to back to a spiritual practice. Even though I really didn't know what Reiki was all about, my intuition said, "Reiki would be a good place to start". It turned out that Reiki covered all the criteria I was looking for. Over a period of seven weeks, I took my Level One and Level Two Reiki Trainings. About six months later, I took the Reiki Master Level Training. The following year, I decided to become a Reiki Master Teacher, after the Universe kept nudging me to do so through repeated client requests. This was not my original intention. I was drawn to it for personal use. Organically my personal work grew into a service business and a way of life.

The initial Reiki training involved learning what Reiki is, its history, self empowerment, practicing meditations, hand positions for energy healing and receiving energy attunements. Advanced levels teach us how to amplify Reiki energy, channel it through ourselves, to others, and through the ethers from a distance. Reiki training can also be a time of shedding old energy and a cleansing of old behavior. It was all of these things for me, plus it felt like something I already knew, like I had been doing it all my life. Like coming home to myself.

Over time, my receptivity to the language of spiritually guided energy awakened more and more. I love using my intuition, creativity and heightened state of awareness to channel positive energy, compassion and truth to my clients. For me, Reiki is a spiritual practice and a way of being. I am Reiki. You are Reiki. We are all made of it. I have found it to be subtle yet powerful, sacred and life changing.

MESSAGES FROM THE PRAYING MANTIS

Divine Timing, Divine Inspiration

Divine Timing Defined

Divine timing is a belief that everything happens exactly when it is supposed to, at the right moment for a specific reason. Nothing can be forced. Patience must be practiced, allowing what will be, to unfold.

How many times have you seen a praying mantis in your lifetime? A few? Not many times ? Can you count how many times on one hand? Or maybe you haven't seen one at all ? Already over a half a century old, I had only seen a few praying mantises in my lifetime. Until the Spring of 2015. There they were again ! Green praying mantises, climbing on the outside of my kitchen window, above the kitchen sink.

The kitchen is where I spend more time than anywhere else in my house. When I'm home, I am often cooking, making tea, washing my hands, or doing dishes at the kitchen sink. The windows in our kitchen overlook our backyard and the neighbors. It is a very pleasant view, with plants, flowers, trees, wooden fences and there is always some wildlife to watch. We see a variety of birds, chipmunks, squirrels, rabbits, deer, foxes and an occasional groundhog. I look out that window over that sink every day, contemplating all matters, big and small. The marble sill under that window serves as a little altar for me, decorated with crystals, shells, mantra stones, and other daily reminders with positive affirmations. I had never seen a praying mantis climbing on that window, or any window, before that summer, and none have come back to that window since. In the evenings, during the weeks I was in the first two Reiki Trainings, I saw praying mantises, sometimes two at a time, hanging out on my kitchen window. Night after night, they would move around the window for hours at a time. I started seeing them in other places too. They began showing up on the front steps of our house and I was astonished to find them in our garbage cans in the garage. How were they getting in there? It was remarkable! The most amazing appearance occurred during the break between Reiki One and Reiki Two. During those weeks, I went on vacation to the beach with my family. One day, I was sitting on our dock, by the water under an umbrella. A praying mantis showed up and hung out with me for hours on top of a big blue canvas umbrella in the sun. It walked down the umbrella and stayed there for a very long time, seemingly staring at me, letting me know it was there, as if to say, "Pay attention!" Another one showed up in a bush right near the umbrella, also making its appearance known for a long time. Again, I had never seen a praying mantis at the shore house before and never since. Pay attention, I did.

Spiritually speaking, the praying mantis is a symbol of stillness, calmness and focus. It represents the power of meditation and introspection. When we see them, they are sending us a message to be still, go within, meditate, to connect with your higher self and your purpose. This insect is a sign that you need to listen to your inner voice, to trust your instincts and to put aside worries and fears. They teach us to have patience and to trust in divine timing. They appear when it's time to take your spiritual practices deeper and to sharpen your clairvoyant abilities. Were these not the exact same reasons I began to study Reiki? Were these messengers speaking to me through the divine order of the universe at just the right time for me to receive them?

This was an exciting and powerful message from an unlikely messenger. Divine timing. Divine inspiration. Divinity speaking to ME, through the praying mantises. My energy was shifting. I didn't know it at the time, but I was opening a door to a world of ancient knowledge and intuitive energy practices that would become an integral part of my work and everyday life. I came to know that I was already a vessel for sharing sacred space, divinely channeled energy, messages and inspiration, for all who are drawn to me.

When I look back, the Universe conspired to make this all happen for me. As I was studying and practicing different modalities of energy healing, opportunities to share Reiki, Vibrational Healing and Meditation started pouring in. It all unfolded effortlessly and aligned with my being. "Your Inner Tranquility" is the business container created for these offerings. The messages from the praying mantises have stayed with me. What they represent have become my daily practices.

GRASSHOPPER MESSAGES – LISTENING TO MY INNER VOICE

Divine Messages In Metaphor

Early on in my practice, I began having visions while offering Reiki to clients. I see things that are "messages in metaphor" for my clients. These messages are always accurate, resonating with each client about a particular issue that is needing attention for their spiritual development. Or they can be appearing to validate information they already know.

By 2019, my energy healing practice was growing fast. I was now teaching Reiki, offering private and group Reiki, Sound Healing and Meditations, on a daily basis. During the summer of 2019, grasshoppers started showing up around me. They would be where I had never seen them before. On the garage door and in the driveway of our home. They would be on my car and stay there while I was driving. One summer day, I had carved out some time for myself. I was home drinking tea on my back porch, which is connected to the kitchen. The same area that the praying mantises showed up. On this particular morning, I was journaling about new ideas for my business. I was brainstorming on paper and meditating about my energy work. My cat was downstairs with me and he kept batting something around. I ignored it for about a half an hour. When I noticed the cat was watching and waiting for something that was on the floor, I finally paid attention. It was a big grasshopper! The grasshopper was staring at the cat and the cat was staring at the grasshopper. I had never seen one in our house in the fifteen years of living there. I picked it up and brought it outside to the backyard garden. When I came back in, I glanced at my computer screen that was sitting on the counter. I didn't scroll to what was on the screen; it was just there. A post about grasshoppers including a big picture of one. This is what the post said: "Grasshoppers can only jump forward, not backward or sideways. This is why the grasshopper is a symbol of good luck all over the world. Grasshopper's ability to connect and understand sound vibrations is why she is also a symbol of your inner voice. She could be telling you to trust yours." Another undeniable, unlikely divine messenger! This messenger was reminding me to trust my inner voice and to trust the" messages in metaphor" that are presented to me.

Here is a tiny sample of divinely guided "messages in metaphor" that have been shown to me while I am facilitating a Reiki session.

∿ I was shown a scene from the view of a spectator at a baseball game, the message being that my client is the spectator of her own life; going through the motions, a little detached, needing to connect to herself and her feelings. This message completely resonated with my client and was exactly what she was feeling inside that needed work. We then explored this metaphor together.

∿ I was shown my client standing up with his younger self standing in front of him. He was looking down on his younger self, with his arm around him. The message was for him to remember his innocence, come back to being playful and have fun. When I relayed this message to my client, he said that he was thinking about this while I was channeling the Reiki. It resonated completely and we then explored this metaphor together.

∿ I was shown an acrobatic formation of people five tiers high. All of the people were focused; holding their positions, perfectly balanced so the whole did not crumble and fall. My client was the only person on the top tier. The message was about finding work-life balance. When I relayed this message, it was exactly what my client was working on. We then explored this metaphor together.

~ I was shown my client as a little girl with her father at a train station in China. He was very loving and held her close to him. It was winter and snowing. When I asked my client about this, it opened up a discussion about her relationship with her father. We had not previously mentioned her father and it turned out to be a relationship that needed attention. We then explored this metaphor together. She could not remember if she had spent time with her father at the train station as a little girl during that session, but after, her father verified that he used to take her to the train station in the winter "all the time"!

~ I was shown my client in a room with four walls. A plain box of a room, no decorations, no windows. The walls were a dusty rose pink. My client was facing herself in the room. She was facing her trauma. The self she was facing was in emotional pain and was bent over. When we discussed this vision, it was exactly what my client was working with; facing her childhood trauma in her adult life. We then explored this metaphor together.

~ I was shown a deep opening, like a well in my client's lower abdomen while I was sending energy to this area. I visualized looking in and the depth of the well continued to get deeper and was unending. The sacral chakra is located two inches below the navel. It is associated with emotional well being, creativity, flexibility, water and pleasure. The message here was to encourage my client to investigate and acknowledge emotional pain, an emotional hole that needed to be filled and to work on emotional flexibility. This story had come up before in our sessions, but this metaphor brought it to light in a new way. We explored this more together and the significance of the sacral energy for her healing journey.

~ I was shown my client dangling in the air above a wide open canyon. I felt very lonely and ungrounded while I was seeing this vision. The message for my client was to acknowledge that she was feeling isolated, lonely and desperately needed grounding. She had not mentioned this to me prior to the session. This message turned out to be extremely pertinent to my client's state of mind and we discussed this metaphor together.

MORE TRAININGS

More Praying Mantises

During the last three months of 2019, I was told by three separate readers; (an astrologer, a palm reader and a medium), who all live in different parts of the country, that I was not using all my power and that I should be studying how to use my psychic ability and mediumship. I was eager to do this and I signed up for classes. Guess who showed up when I began these training sessions? The praying mantises. This time they were brown, instead of green. They began coming to the garage door and while I was working in the garden, they appeared next to me. I loved seeing them again, confirming the divine connection we all have to the cosmic order of the Universe.

Listen, Align, Flow

ly Practice

..t.

Go within.

Be still.

Listen to your higher self.

Sense the energy around you.

Make friends with unlikely messengers.

Trust your instincts.

Love yourself, All beings and Mother Earth.

Relish what makes you distinctive.

Practice gratitude.

Be patient.

Find magic in the mundane.

Let go of what weighs you down.

Do what makes you happy.

Spread kindness.

Live intentionally.

Listen, Align, Flow.

~ Divinity Speaking ~

"Smile at yourself. Celebrate the collage of your attributes and experiences, rendering you beautifully unique. This is the love language of your divinity."

ABOUT THE AUTHOR

CAROL LOUISE SCHOFFMANN

Carol Schoffmann is the founder of Your Inner Tranquility. She is an Intuitive Reiki Master Teacher, Sound Healing Practitioner, Meditation Teacher and Spiritual Guide.Carol helps her clients find peace, balance, purpose and joy in their everyday life. Clients love her signature "Mind, Body, Spirit Tune-Ups", combining her knack for putting people at ease, space holding abilities and energy therapies. She teaches her clients to celebrate what is uniquely beautiful about themselves and to embody the art of living authentically.

Carol has facilitated over 2000 Reiki, Sound Healing, Meditation and Teaching Sessions. She has been featured on the "Bearth" and "Talking Joy" podcasts.

Carol is a single Mom by choice. She lives happily in New Jersey with her amazing daughter, Mita, their dog, Jack and kitties Boo and Snowflake.

Website: https://www.yourinnertranquility.com

Facebook: Your Inner Tranquility

Instagram: @yourinnertranquility

Email: carol@yourinnertranquility.com

9

MY BODY IS MY COMPASS

ELISHA GREENLEAF

"*Y*our body is fighting itself."

This has been the answer to the question "what caused the rheumatoid arthritis?" The same answer for the last fifteen years from every 'western medicine' rheumatologist I have seen. No doctor outside my Ayurvedic Doctor can explain to me why or where the rheumatoid arthritis came from. How is that possible? Oh right, there's no money for *Big Pharma* if you're healthy.

I knew, deep in my soul, there had to be another way to handle this dreadful diagnosis: rheumatoid arthritis (ra) at the age of twenty-one.

I was sitting in my 2007 Phantom Purple Mica Mazda 3 talking to my dad 3000 miles across the country back in NH... sitting in my car with the sunshade up, blocking the hot Arizona sun, as I balled my eyes out. Feeling so much resentment to the universe for doing this *to me*! This was the worst life sentence I could have received.

We're talking DEEP victim mentality and shame around this prognosis. The doctor informed me that there was no cure for ra. I would be dealing with pain for the rest of my life, likely be on disability and wheelchair bound by the time I was thirty. Thankfully my father did what fathers do, and did his best to be positive and support me the best he could through the phone. Blurting out his plan to come and help me figure this out ASAP.

After the initial shock, I decided to get a second opinion because I felt I had lost all power to the doctor who announced this horrible prognosis. Deep down I knew something else was true. My poor body was so weak and worn down. I just didn't have it in me to fight or question. I chose to go to another doctor and start again. She was a little more positive with, "sometimes it goes into remission if we layer the medication properly." Even in this state of confusion, a red flag arose. 'Layering of medication?' "WTF does that mean?" I blurted out at her.

She explained: Starting with steroids, methotrexate, then add on a TNF blocker and even pain pills to get more relief. And since these medications have side effects, they added another drug that helps calcium absorption. Which tasted like the nastiest chocolate ever eaten, was chewy and got stuck in my teeth... horrendous. I began to wonder if the side effects of the medication I was taking were worse than the actual dis-ease. So the methotrexate, pain pills and chocolate calcium lasted about a week since I was either sick to my stomach, vomiting and/or dizzy.

At this point, I disassociated from my body. I was working full time and going to school. I felt so alone because there was no one my age who I knew, who had anything like this. And when I told people what I had, they would say, "oh arthritis, like old people have?" which made me feel even shittier.

So at the age of twenty-one, I was depressed, alone, and feeling totally unsupported because once I took the steroids most of the physical symptoms went away. For years I never really told people, except in my closest circle, what I was silently going through. People just knew me as the healthy girl because I was eating so cleanly...

otherwise I might get a flare meaning my body would get inflamed and hurt – a lot.

It's frustrating to look back to this twenty-one year-old version of me who was so broken, disconnected, and unloved. I looked for love in men instead of myself. I wanted a man to love me in a way I didn't know how to love myself. And because I didn't know my own truth, I'd blame them for not being who I thought they were when we started dating. Finding the smallest, stupidest thing to get mad at, I'd blow it up and break up with them.

I spent a good part of my twenties trying to find the magical doctor, modality or procedure that would cure the ra. Again, despite what every rheumatologist told me I knew there were answers! I tried everything from chiropractic, massage, acupuncture, energy work, leech therapy, colonics, gluten free, dairy free, nightshade free diets, sauna, naturopathic, High Dose Vitamin Protocols, Herbs, Network Chiropractic... It was all so overwhelming.

I worked with so many teachers and 'support' along the way. As I look back, divinity spoke to me at all times. Sometimes I listened, sometimes I didn't.

Almost every time I went to the rheumatologist, it would be a new face because the last guy always wanted to push their agenda on me. Never listening to my needs and desires. Telling me I was wrong and my desire to manage the ra with nutrition, yoga and other modalities would not help. According to them, only their prescribed medications would work.

For about five years I was on auto-pilot. Doing what I needed to survive. I was having a lot of sex with a lot of guys because in those moments of orgasmic ecstasy I felt alive in my body. For that split second I was able to feel something other than pain. I would feel 'love.' It was very external and conditional. At the time I thought I was loving myself but looking back at it, it wasn't love, it was covering a dark hole I wasn't willing to look at. It kept me safe because it was just about sex and getting f*cked... (literally and figuratively as I later realized). I didn't have to open my heart; I could keep the walls up. Walls from when my mom left when I was six and when I got my heart broken from my high school sweetheart at the age of sixteen.

Then I found someone who mirrored me. I knew deep in my soul it wouldn't work but I had to dive into this committed relationship because there was a sense of safety. It filled that yearning to be loved.

Then around my twenty-ninth birthday I had a really bad pain in my left knee and woke up with a huge cyst behind my knee. I went to the doctor and was told, "It is part of the ra. As you get older things like that will happen more frequently." I was frustrated, angry and began to feel a lot of guilt and shame for ignoring my body for the last eight years, suppressing the symptoms with medication.

That was when I knew deep in my soul the reason I had ra was to show the world it was possible to heal my body. If a woman can grow a baby in her body for nine months, why couldn't I reverse the disease within my body?

As divinity spoke through me and I was beginning to pay more attention to the signs pointing me in the right direction. A friend who was told she couldn't become pregnant, was able to conceive a baby within six months of starting the protocol. So I decided to call her Practitioner. She spoke to me in a way that resonated so deeply in my soul she started to give me answers I had never received from any western doctor. Finally I thought I found the solution. I spent the next year getting off the steroids and TNF blockers. I was finally free of western medication, my dream since the original diagnosis. I was managing with the food I ate; No cow dairy, wheat and only high enzyme foods. I was finally repairing my gut. Plus taking lots of herbs to repair and nurture my system along with doing Emotion Code. Overall, I was doing very well. Even though I had lost a lot of weight from the changes in meds, I was finally caring for myself in a whole new way.

Then that 'oh so new and fun' relationship from a few years ago took a turn when he held up a mirror for me. Looking back on it... everything he did that upset me was a reflection of something in myself I didn't like or had disassociated from years ago. Most of his friends were females which brought up so much jealousy in me. I realized this stemmed from all those years ago when my dad was dating women and gave more attention to them and I became the 'third wheel.' A normal family dynamic, but when I went from having 100% of dad's attention because I am an only child to only 50%, it was an issue that suppressed my true feelings. I wanted to be perfect for my dad and not be like 'my mom' or 'most women'.

So, as we fell into each other's emotional traumas our relationship declined. I began to be dismissive and distant. Resenting him, being jealous and finally having him ask me "if I still loved him?" "No." Here we go again with another relationship not working. But then I had an epiphany. I was at the center of every relationship that hadn't worked out. I was part of the problem. It was my internal world that was creating these situations to happen in my external world.

Finding My Inner Goddess

The end of that relationship led me to a whole new beginning for the first time in my life. As I was living in my own apartment, I began to really look at who I was? What were my dreams? What did I want to accomplish in my life? And how was I going to once and for all heal from the ra?

So began my introduction to Breathwork. More time to attend yoga classes. Spending time relaxing in a way that truly nourished my exhausted and overwhelmed nervous system. I went that entire year without a TV. I read a lot. I got so much clearer on who I was. I began to realize the trauma from my childhood, which I had suppressed, was surfacing. I also became very clear - my 'why' was to share my experience with the world so no woman has to feel as unsupported as I did.

I even met a very kind man who was nothing like my wish list desires. The complete opposite of any other man I had ever dated. He supported me in a way I had never felt before. He voluntarily asked to go to the rheumatologist with me and pushed me to go to the best that I had dreamed of going to despite being 'out of network' and pricey.

I intuitively knew that I had to keep looking at my options until I found a doctor who at least would listen to me. That came the day I went to Dr. Howard. He finally listened to my needs and desires. However, he also asked for me to reciprocate. Wow, this was all new for me.

So I shared my story, tears running down my face, and my beautiful partner Tank, held my hand as I began to release ten years of feeling so unsupported.

I listened to what he had to say!! After the last three years of completely being off ra medications and doing the 100% herbal route, that too had taken a huge toll on my body. My fingers had begun to become disfigured, I had lost so much weight (I was down to 8olbs) and I was still in pain and experiencing inflammation. Here I was fighting my body yet again and not listening to all the signs of dis-ease because I was taking the healthy route which I took a very strong stance on.

This was the crossroads for me to understand an even deeper balance. As Dr. Howard explained, we needed to use western medicine to reduce the current flare state, while I continued doing all the healthy modalities. He explained how we could integrate it all and work to wean off western medicine eventually but it was vital to my physical being to intervene with the drugs I had sworn away only a few years earlier.

This allowed me the best of both worlds. My body flourished with this new integration. This was the beginning of a whole new realization for me since most of my life had been extremes.

He mentioned a new drug in pill form instead of shots... This made me feel so much better because I knew my body. I could easily digest this since I was now setting intentions with any food, herb, or vitamin that went into my body.

As I started taking this new drug, I wrote on the bottle, "health, love, compassion, forgiveness." I wanted to make sure the energy of this pill was as high as possible. Over the next month I came back to life. I was gaining weight. I was feeling less pain and I finally got the courage to go to a yoga class and even decided to take Yoga Teacher Training.

This doctor showed me a new perspective. I had always thought it was a fight. It had to be this OR that. But he helped me see a way of integrating two opposing sides. It allowed my body to integrate the polarization that was taking place physically and mentally in my body.

My new partner, Tank, supported me when I told him I would be dedicating my weekends to training for almost nine months. A lot of old programs came up that he would leave me or cheat on me. As I spent the next nine months going through teacher training, the pandemic hit. The weekend everything shut down in March of 2020 I was at a silent retreat for the Kundalini Yoga Teacher Training. I made a pact to myself that within the next year I would be teaching Yoga Full Time. I was done with corporate America! And divinity spoke to me yet again; I had a voicemail on the very next day from my boss who said, "I'm sorry to let you know you have been furloughed for at least a month." My prayers had been answered. It was time for me to start my own business. Thinking this would be an easy endeavor I took the first month to just relax and let my body flow into this new routine. Then Daisy, my shih tzu of fourteen years, who was like my daughter passed away.

I took an emotional hit, but I realized I could focus on my business 100% without interruption so I decided to get certified in Emotion Code and Body Code.

Thankfully with all this extra time on my hands I was really able to focus on my health and healing. In June of 2020, for the first time in over a decade, my lab work came back showing all the markers for ra were in the normal range. Wait, so it was as easy as focusing my time on ME? What a blessing I received. Not at all how I thought it was going to look, but that is the beautiful thing with divinity, it almost never looks the way we want or think it will.

Now I knew it was time to go full steam ahead to make my company 'Bee the Glow' a huge success. But you know as divinity would have it.... It didn't work out that way. I began Breath Facilitator Training from my longtime Teacher, Zach. This began to reveal an even deeper level of trauma and cultural conditioning. So I spent the next year really working on myself even more, creating a deeper connection with my soul even with those parts of me I had disliked and pushed away for so long.

I knew this was an integral part of my healing and began sharing this work with the world. I watched not only myself but my clients transform to new levels I never even expected to see happen. One client decided to buy a boat and live on the ocean. He began to embody the oneness we all dream of connecting with. Another took back her power, learned to set boundaries like she had never done before, transforming her life and relationships. Another began to feel in her body and connect even deeper to her inner knowing magically transforming her life.

Then I got comfortable. I started to go back to the busy life, old patterns, not eating as healthily as I desired and the ra slowly creeped back. But this time I had greater awareness and knew it wasn't what I thought it was. I began to dig even deeper into my parent's divorce, previous relationships and life choices and how it was affecting me on a much deeper level.

It was frustrating but it allowed me to look even deeper in the safety I found within the dis-ease! And then came the question: Who would I be without this condition? The ra has shaped my life and divinely guided me through the past fifteen years and continues to guide me to look at what I need to release to get to the next level. The times my left hand hurts and I uncover some deeper understanding, I realize it's not about the ra diagnosis or prognosis. It is that I have turned my body into its own compass to show me what to do next. How to stay in my flow and follow my divine guidance to make a larger impact in my life, community, family, and the world. I have no idea if the ra will ever be gone 'medically', but I do know that the symptoms of it will disappear as I continue to clear out the subconscious garbage that I have picked up from my environment.

I also know that the diagnosis fifteen years ago reminded me of my soul's mission in the world to illuminate the innate healing potential in myself and each and every soul I meet. My physical body is here on this journey with me, always showing my next step. And do I choose to listen to it? Yes I do! And I hope you do too. You are your best advocate. Don't let anyone take that away from you! Listen to your body, believe in your body. It is here supporting you every moment despite what those around you may say.

~ *Divinity Speaking* ~
"You take out the garbage regularly so your house doesn't stink! But when was the last time you dumped your subconscious garbage?"

ABOUT THE AUTHOR

ELISHA GREENLEAF

Elisha Greenleaf is the Founder of Bee the Glow. She helps entrepreneurial women break cycles of dis-ease and transform generational trauma. She guides women back to their Inner Goddess through Breathwork, The Emotion Code™, The Body Code™, Kundalini Yoga and all things woo!

She lives by the motto, "You take out the garbage regularly so your house doesn't stink! But when was the last time you dumped your subconscious garbage?"

She has helped 100's of women since her diagnosis of Rheumatoid Arthritis over 15 years ago as she guides them to reconnect with what they already have within themselves that they have forgotten over a lifetime of cultural programming.

She lives in Scottsdale, AZ with her partner in life, Tank, who is a magician and their pomchi, Pennie.

Website: www.beetheglow.com/divinity-speaks
Facebook: www.facebook.com/BeetheGlow
Instagram: @beetheglow.breathwork

10

DANCING WITH THE DIVINE

EMILY REIMANN

I have always known that there was something I was meant to do; a feeling that has been with me as a driving force my entire life. I remember wondering, at a very young age, what my purpose was on this planet and how I could discover it. I did not really understand where this thought came from, but I knew it would be my mission in life to discover this purpose and follow the path.

Although I had this inner drive, I never knew which direction to go in. I based my decisions solely on intuition, feelings, signs, and often sought advice from others. In middle school, I discovered a book on yoga and meditation and began to practice in my room.

During my meditations I would go deep and imagine myself becoming one with the earth, connecting to what I now consider my spirit and the cosmic web that connects us all. I would feel my physical body dissolve, and experience a sensation of connectedness to the elements around me as well as the natural world.

Ever since then I have had an interest in holistic medicine. I became very conscientious regarding what I ate, how I lived, and how I moved my body. Over the years, I had many ideas of what I wanted to be when I "'grew up.'" I looked into a variety of careers that always had a common theme: helping people heal and get more in tune with their body in a holistic way.

This theme showed up when I first considered pursuing physical therapy and nutrition. However, when I looked into these options, my intuition guided me otherwise. I followed this nudge and instead found myself attending a school that had nothing to do with the majors I had first considered, and it was exactly where I was meant to be. My undergraduate experience is where I first had the opportunity to be on my own and I spent those years connecting deeply to nature, spirituality, and eastern philosophy.

As my spiritual development progressed, I began to dive even deeper into the world of yoga and energy healing. About two years after college, I moved back home to New Jersey and went through a rebirthing process. I became a certified yoga instructor, started attending Reiki certification trainings, and began teaching yoga and offering energy healing sessions. I also began to receive acupuncture regularly during this time.

This world brought me to my mentor, my acupuncturist. I remember the moment I called in a mentor so clearly. I was practicing yoga at my favorite studio and was struck with a moment of clarity and inspiration. I asked the universe for a clear direction, because I knew I needed something more. Shortly after, my acupuncturist called and offered me a job as his office manager. My soul said yes, and I accepted the position immediately.

I spent many years working with him and assisted him as he built his practice here in New Jersey. I learned not only how to run an office, but my understanding of health and well-being transformed. I shifted tremendously during this time and became much more grounded. When he suggested I go to school to become licensed, I was resistant to the idea, as I still felt like I had some healing to do.

It wasn't until a few years later when things fell into place. I realized that Chinese Medicine and acupuncture were the *perfect* combination of everything I had ever been interested in. It is a union of the physical, mental, emotional, and spiritual aspects of a person. Most importantly, I felt ready to embark on this journey as I knew it would change me completely.

The path towards becoming licensed was a challenging one, and there were many tests along the way, both literally and figuratively. After the first year or so of my master's program, I began to feel a huge shift, and not a positive one. I entered into what I now consider one of my darkest times. Every negative feeling I had ever felt in life resurfaced during this time for deeper healing. This was a death and rebirth cycle where I learned the true meaning of perseverance. I graduated and became licensed in September of 2019.

I began to practice at the office where I had worked for many years, but something still did not feel quite right. Even though I had the support of my mentor and the patients who had come to know me, I felt a nudge to be out on my own. I waited, and as I did, I prayed to know when the time was right. Shortly after we began to experience the effects of the COVID pandemic.

I knew the universe was opening a door for me, and for the entire world. My boss and I began to discuss the options and came to the conclusion that it would make the most sense for me to take time off. I kid you not, on the last day of work there, one of the patients I was treating offered me a space to rent in her yoga studio. I knew this was what I had been asking for, so I said yes and, shortly after, became an LLC to begin to see my own patients.

Here is where I began to blend all of the tools I had learned in a completely new way, and I began to open up more to my divine channel. I incorporated energy healing into my acupuncture treatments as well as essential oils, mindfulness, and guided meditation. It was slow to build as we were still navigating the effects of the pandemic, and I often wondered if this was the right time.

I loved the work, but was not making enough to support myself. During the pandemic I had been staying with my partner and his elderly grandfather, whom he was helping to care for, and struggled quite a bit. I eventually made the decision to move out on my own and I went through another death and rebirth cycle.

I considered what to do next, as my private practice was not providing me with the support I needed to live on my own, and began to apply for positions at acupuncture studios. I was very selective with where I applied, because I did not want to take just any job. I wanted something where I could continue to grow as a practitioner and feel connected to my patients. I wanted to be in a space that incorporated the spiritual and emotional aspects of this medicine.

I found an opening in Jersey City that looked promising and applied; shortly after I was offered the position. This time, I leaned on the signs of my guides for confirmation and received this information through angel numbers and synchronicities.

It is funny how divine timing works. I would have never applied to this position before for a number of reasons, yet I knew on a deep level that taking this position would ultimately benefit my future practice. Even though it would appear as if I was shelving my ultimate vision and walking away.

I realized that my vision and how I desired to hold space for my patients was still in its infant stage, and I knew that taking this job would actually benefit me and my patients in the long run. I accepted this calling from spirit, and have grown as a practitioner. I found ways to connect to an entirely different population, and learned more about what my soul desires to create moving forward.

During this time, I have practiced surrendering to flow even more and have worked instead on shifting my frequency. I learned that as I shift and recalibrate, that I attract the things that my soul desires. And I learned how to shift in order to energetically hold and contain these things. I became more fully empowered in myself, my mission, and the work that I am here on this earth to do.

My work is still growing and evolving, and I have begun to practice the private sessions I have crafted again on those closest in my circle. I am now able to give deeper sessions that blend acupuncture, energy healing, essential oils, and channeling. I have offered these sessions in person as well as remotely, through the instructed use of acupressure. More recently, I have been collaborating and networking with local groups who I feel are more aligned with my soul's mission.

I have also recently connected with a woman who has offered a local space to practice in, yet again, but I know now that there is no rush. Everything happens in divine timing, and I trust this process whole-heartedly. What is meant for you will come, and there is no need to force it to happen.

Finding your path isn't always an easy one, but I can tell you that every experience you have builds upon the one before. There are always lessons to learn and grow, and once you begin to open yourself up and lean on this belief, your whole world begins to shift. Take the journey that is best for you, and trust the process.

~ Divinity Speaking ~
'Divinity is a dance between inspiration and action; between surrendering, being open, and stepping forward. How you choose to dance is up to you."

ABOUT THE AUTHOR

EMILY REIMANN

Emily Reimann is a licensed acupuncturist, healer, and spiritual channel. She has been honing her skills in the alternative healthcare field for almost a decade, when she first became a certified yoga instructor. She completed a number of trainings in energy healing prior to studying Chinese Medicine. She uses her knowledge and intuition to create unique and personalized treatments.

Emily helps individuals who are looking to develop a more intimate connection with themselves in order to heal on a deep level. She is gifted at integrating the physical, mental, emotional, and spiritual aspects of an individual and is passionate about mental health as well as women's health issues. She also helps individuals shift their experience of pain, whether it be an acute or chronic condition. She is an expert space holder with a kind and compassionate heart. Currently she resides in northern New Jersey with her sweet yet, vocal Maine Coon cat and spends her free time in nature.

Website: www.emilyreimann.com

Instagram: @naturalwellnesswithemily

Email: contact@emilyreimann.com

11

OF THE LEARNING

HEATHER O'NEILL

THE LISTENING

As I sit at my desk, enveloped in the space of the morning's stillness, the window slightly cracked open, I can hear the birds singing. Other than the occasional airplane sound slicing through the sky it is quiet and peaceful. I can see the soft rustle of the breeze move through the trees and as I soak it all in I acknowledge that this is Divinity speaking.

This particular morning a friend sent me the daily lesson from her 'A Course In Miracles' workbook. The lesson was on sickness as defense in the body. She sent it because I had not been feeling well for a couple of days. As a Reiki practitioner and an HSP (Highly Sensitive Person) & empath, I knew that my work was to figure out the energetics underneath me feeling out of alignment with my well-being. I dug into what was going on in my current circumstances to further understand myself and what I might be defending against.

But as I read the lesson, the clarity was slow in coming. I wasn't finding any obvious issue that I felt I was in defense of, but I knew that I just had yet to discover it. This happens sometimes as my human self melds with my highest self in search of answers for healing. And when they are not always immediate, I don't worry because I know all I have to do is ask for help.

Because Divinity speaks to us all the time, every day, in myriad ways. We don't always trust in this because sometimes we don't know how to listen. Perhaps we don't even realize that we aren't listening. As spirits having a human experience that chose to forget who and what we really are, we could be making enough noise in our minds that we render ourselves incapable of truly hearing.

We can do this often and unknowingly all the while fooling ourselves into thinking we are ripe with awareness when we are not. It's a forked path, where one side has us believing that we are open and attentive to our signs and messages, while the other side embodies a deafness that simply leaves us in the space of "we don't know what we don't know."

But both forks can fool us. And it is up to us to be ever mindful of truly listening.

One of the greatest gifts we can give to another person is intent listening. And truly hearing what the Divine is saying is the greatest gift we can give to ourselves   .

It may not feel that way sometimes because the mind can be sneaky and allow us to hear only what the ego says, even so far as to convince us that IT is the Divine, but alas it is not. And we may come to question the places we end up in and the people that surround us. We wonder why the work we do does not fulfill, why the true desires in our heart do not manifest. Not knowing that it's the result of not knowing our own self.

Because within ourselves is where we can genuinely hear the Divine. It's a matter of becoming quiet enough to practice the discernment of what we hear and see as the messages from Spirit sent to direct us on

our paths. Instead sometimes we get stuck in expectation, w
our messages to be 'loud and clear' and then mistaking the
definition of loud and having clarity look different than we thought
would.

Yes sometimes synchronicity is beautifully and wonderfully obvious, but this happens when we are most in alignment with God. And we cannot fully hear God if we do not know ourselves. Sometimes we are taught that God is outside of us, someplace far away in the ether. But God is right next to us at all times, within us since the moment of our creation, the fabric of the souls that inhabit our physical bodies. The folly is to keep us disconnected from self, disconnected from the necessary quiet and stillness with which lead us right to God. Because it's in that place where our eyes truly see and our hearts truly hear what Divinity is saying.

THE HEARING

It is constant, all-encompassing speech, but not the kind we are accustomed to when we think of talking. Sometimes Divinity speaks to us through others as the messenger. And we can become adept at really listening to what those around us are saying to us, knowing this is a modality. But as the Word has formed the earth, trees, birds and I who listens, this speech is one that is not only heard but felt. It's a listening via our spirit. A knowing that all we have to do is open ourselves up to the connection that has **never** left us, even though we may have convinced ourselves of such.

When we open our heart center, the connection is vibrant and rich. The heart must be directing the mind, which should not be in the driver's seat. The mind is not to be ignored, but rather approached with temperance. Not as gospel, but as suggestion and exploration, never assuming that everything it has to say is truth.

We can allow our minds to take us down if we are not careful, which is why the heart center, whose electric beating is also of the

ind, was created with the same biological
t we come to know God and the many, many
to speak to us. They come in the form of other
e, music, numbers, timelines, colors, sounds,

also in alignment with our overall vibration. When I am clear and connected to love and joy and the higher frequencies, life flows through me with seeming effortless ease. I did not always live this way, but after many years of spiritual practice and focusing intently on raising my vibration, I can know my Divine pictures and ideas of inspired action with much more clarity. Manifestations appear more quickly, and instead of focusing on what it is I want, I sit in the space of love, gratitude, goodness and Godliness and set my intentions on doing the things that keep me aligned with that space.

It's like the dial on a radio. I choose actions that turn my dial into the Divine. I practice compassion for others, keep my heart open in love even if I am experiencing anger, and I acknowledge fully that I desire to act from my higher self and to flow with the will of the highest Creator.

This is an important step. And it was the biggest game changer for me upon my first level awakening while going through my divorce. I remember the moment with distinct clarity, as if it was yesterday, even though it was over eleven years ago. I was at the lowest point I had been in my life. What I had defined myself with had crumbled around me. I was young and immature and did not yet possess the knowing that this was a gift. That in breakdown can come the most magical of breakthrough and rebirth. And as I laid in my bed one night in utter despair, devoid of hope of ever feeling better and resigned to a bland life that thankfully my child kept me anchored to, I looked up at the ceiling and said aloud **"Thy will be done."**

Everything shifted after that. And while perhaps not instantaneously, it was then that my true healing began.

Not long after that night I was scheduled to go to a convention for a network marketing business I had at the time. My Gram, who I was very close to, had recently transitioned and I was completely empty. Again in my naivety I did not realize the value of that emptiness and the power in the choice of what gets filled from that space. I remember telling my mom before I was to travel that I didn't think I could do it. That I had nothing to give to anyone. Again not inner-standing that within NO-thing is the most expansive place of possibility.

My mom, who is also highly intuitive, told me that she had a feeling that this trip was actually going to be very good for me. She felt I needed to go, that somehow it would be truly beneficial for me. So I trusted in her Mama-wisdom and went. And she was right.

On that trip I was reintroduced to my personal power. I heard motivational speakers for the first time in my life. I was presented with perspectives that removed me from the space of having BECOME my pain. It had been my identity up until that moment where I was awakening to the fact that it didn't have to be. In fact it shouldn't be!

Spending so much time in low vibration had built up momentum that had been taking me further and further down. And I had lost any sight of the choice I had in reclaiming my own power, in telling different stories, and in being new. But I was reminded that in every NOW moment is the possibility of a NEW me. And I was blown away by one of the speakers, a Christian man who read bible quotes like I had never heard them before. Shining light on the strength that we all possess, he reminded us that we are not weak, but that we walk with the power of the Divine within us at all times. I was reconnected to my spirit through Spirit. It was like these words describing The

WORD plucked me out of a deep dark hole and put me back onto solid ground in the light.

I was listening to Divinity speak to me loud and clear and I was taught how to hear it again.

THE PRACTICING

My entire life I've had a personal relationship with God. It has never been a religion directed relationship as I have never been one to enjoy restrictions and rules or being told how I HAD to do something. I am a typical Aquarian who likes to do things her own way. A bit off the beaten path, turned off to doing or buying or saying what everyone else was doing just to fit in. Looking back, I have never really fit in in that way, and at this point on my path I am not only happy about that but I embrace it. I live through my essence, my own energetic signature, and I can fully feel it now and I love who I am. I love that Self through my relationship with the Divine. I love that Self as a spirit created by Spirit.

The same way that my mother and father are within my blood and bones is the same way the Divine Mother & Father are woven through the fabric of my soul. And that relationship comes with both honoring and surrendering. So while I had been honoring my whole life, I had not truly surrendered until that day I looked up at my bedroom ceiling and spoke that phrase. Along with the "I am", which speaks into existence the energy to form matter, "Thy Will Be Done" is a key with which our human selves LET the Divine know we are truly ready to listen when spoken to.

After that moment and that convention trip the student was ready and the teachers appeared. The words I still needed to hear began to be said by the spiritual guides and thought leaders I was introduced to. The classes I was meant to take that held just the exact learning that I needed appeared in my path, and I said yes to it all with wonder and amazement.

But how do we get there and stay there became my next inquiries.

Meditation, prayer, asking, listening, allowing and tending to my vibration were the answers. Cultivating a practice of sitting quietly and going within serves more than will be highlighted in these words. Visualizing what we want and the things we pray for lets Divinity know what we desire. Journaling, speaking, putting energy behind our words and the stories we tell lets Life Force know what we want to create. We were created with the energy that created all that is. We emerged from the Word. And thus we too can use the word in conversation with Spirit.

We can forget this sometimes, when things don't go our way. When stuff doesn't turn out how we want it to, it can be easy to think no one is listening. But those are the times we need to intently tune in, as it's most likely US who is not doing the listening.

God is love, the highest vibration there is. If you ever want to see and feel that, watch little children play. Young kids generally live in the space of that connection before life has its way with them if they are not given the proper tools to stay conscious.

This is why so many of us are met with the need to do inner child work when we embark on the path of personal & spiritual growth and awakening. There are pieces of us that either don't move past childhood experiences or that also need to be brought into our adulting life.

One of the teachers that was brought into my journey after that amazing trip had written a book called *Find Your Fire at Forty* . As God spoke through serendipity, the author's name was the same as mine. And it resonated with me on so many levels. I was also forty at the time and hadn't yet wrangled the aging stuff to a comfortable place. But the biggest transformation came from an exercise she proposed within those pages that was simple yet SO profound in the shift it elicited. She suggested that as we are searching for our life's purpose, we make a list of all the things we used to enjoy doing as a child. The immense take away was the wonderment of WHY we ever left those things behind.

Do we come to believe later in life that we are no longer deserving of wild abandonment and joy? Of simply deciding in the moment what lights us up or of the importance of following our highest excitement? In childhood and through the teens we seem more likely to follow what we are passionate about. What we are "in the mood" to do. Our mood IS our vibration. And our soul KNOWS the frequency we are meant to be in. In fact, Life will continually bring us experiences to jar us out of low mode when we are not in alignment with our soul's purpose and highest vibration.

Sometimes they are awful, traumatic and painful so that we become AWARE of our state of being and become conscious around wanting something different. Sometimes Life brings us what we need to grow through, and when we don't yet get it we will continually be given the opportunity to do so. And one of the most beautiful ways to help us recalibrate to our soul's essence is to recall what lit us up as children. Grateful to this namesake author and her book for being my messenger, I set about making my list. It contained simple things like reading, and things that bring me immense pleasure and joy like singing and dancing. Things that I had gotten away from, things I told myself I no longer had time for.

Our minds are wily, and they can convince us of age-ism. Lying to us about the things we were once passionate about no longer being appropriate for us. But as I made that list, I could actually feel into the lightness of the things on it. It shifted me. I remembered. I made a commitment to my inner child to still care for her. To show her love by doing things she enjoys. My highest self reminded all facets of me that we all make up this current incarnation and that I am worthy of love, excitement, passion, and joyful experiences. And I can assure you that sitting wrapped in a comfy blanket reading with a warm cup of tea brings me immense joy!

I am so grateful for the life experiences I have encountered. I am grateful that through my dark night of the soul the true light at the end of the tunnel found me. I am grateful that I was willing to let go and let God. And I am grateful that Divinity has never really left my side, I had just forgotten how to listen.

I had been engaging life through the false beliefs that years of unconscious living had enabled me to create. I don't fault myself for that. I know that I chose to forget when I chose to come into this lifetime   . I acknowledge that the journey here is one of remembrance and that the pathway is through deeply knowing myself. I greatly appreciate all of the life experiences I have had that allow me to meet me again and again and again. I have become a student of my own thinking and from that place of observation I have seen many things that good, bad and ugly labels could apply to.

But I know they are a matter of learning. The journey of coming back home within the heart. To the place where the Creator lives within us always. To the "I am" as the spirit having the human experience. And it's from there that I can hear.

~ *Divinity Speaking* ~
"The true space of listening is in the surrender. The true path to God is to know thyself. It is there we can truly hear when Divinity speaks.
"

ABOUT THE AUTHOR

HEATHER O'NEILL

Heather O'Neill is the Owner of Heather O'Neill Inner Healing. She is an Energy Healer and Energy Alignment Coach. Heather is also an intuitive empath whose life mission embraces natural healing and raising the collective vibration. As a Reiki Master Teacher, she moves clients into inner balance to facilitate mental, emotional & physical healing and general well-being. She works with clients both in person as well as virtually. As a coach, she specializes in working with empaths on understanding their sensitivity & energy field and practicing good energetic hygiene. Being an empath mentor, she guides her clients to see their emotional depth as a gift. Heather is also a certified hypnotist and Human Design practitioner. Her podcast Conscious Conversations can be found on Rumble. She is passionate about being a mom, dancing, spending time in nature, meditation, love, laughter and conscious living in alignment with our Creator.

Website: www.Heatheroneillinnerhealing.com

Facebook: www.facebook.com/EnergyHealerHeather

Instagram: @heather_oneill_inner_healing

Podcast - Conscious Conversations: www.rumble.com/c/c-867287

12

DIVINE MOTHER

HEATHER ROBINSON

I could tell you numerous examples and stories of when the divine was clearly speaking to me, through me, or communicating with me. Where my guides or God or the universe or whoever intervened and influenced my life in clear and potent ways, and I knew in that moment divine energy was present and guiding me.

Like when I prayed to God at thirteen that if He was real then the flower I left on my windowsill would still be alive after a week of being away for my grandmother's funeral and it having already been the lone survivor of the bouquet that was weeks old.

Like when I was walking out of my room having had no thought prior to this moment of paranoia or insecurity and had a crystal-clear message to "look at his phone" and found texts that let me know we were done.

Like when I asked my guides for help to figure out whether to stay in California and have my baby without any support, or to move home and be with family, and that night I was woken up randomly at 5am and went to find my baby's father naked with another woman in the back of her car.

Like when my guides showed me posts about a multi-author book project twelve times in an hour so it would click and I'd finally think, "Hmm, I could do that!"

I have believed in the divine since I was a young child and could grasp the subject. I have a core memory that has probably come to be the most profound experience of my entire life in establishing my spirituality.

I remember being with my parents and my brother in the car, backing out of the driveway. The same music as always was playing, and I was looking out the window at my house as we backed out. When we stopped in the cul-de-sac to then shift it in drive, time stopped. I left my body, and also was more "in" my body than ever.

My awareness of my soul emerged, and questions poured in.

"What am I doing here?"

"Why am I in THIS body? In this family? In this house? In this part of the world? Why did I choose THIS life?"

A simple experience, a small child pondering life.

But once I became pregnant and needed to satiate my desire for understanding the portal of bringing a soul earth side, I read the first book that ever really landed for me spiritually, and I realized the significance of this memory.

My soul was remembering I came here for a reason, and couldn't remember that reason, naturally, and brought awareness of the question to my human mind.

It took another twenty years to figure out some of those answers to the questions I asked that day, but it's all divinely connected.

Despite a strong belief throughout my life, and despite experiences of strong and clear connection with the divine, before the recent months, I still wouldn't say I've had the strongest connection with the divine. I couldn't see or feel God in my life, I didn't understand the power in prayer, and I don't feel like my intuition has been strong or trustworthy for most of my life.

Why? Because there were so many other experiences where I followed my intuition and it didn't work out, so many instances I prayed and wasn't answered, so much disconnection and trauma had been present that I can't say I've really been in tune with my intuition or connected to God and the divine much at all.

Divine energy is God. We are all simply a reflection of God, God lives in us all, and we have access to divine energy just by being human. Trauma disconnects us from ourselves, our truth, the truth that we are whole and perfect just as we are. As a result, we are disconnected from God, and from divine energy. They are still present, and they still have influence when we're disconnected, but we aren't in our power to feel it, work together, and use the connection well. Many of us spend our entire lives trying to find something to fill that void, to feel connected, to fix ourselves so we can be whole again.

I've been disconnected from my body, my intuition, and God for most of my life. I've lived in my trauma, not believing I was enough, or worthy, or knowing what unconditional love was or how to give it to myself. I experienced a lot of pain because of my trauma and disconnection.

When I reflect on my personal experiences, both those that were clearly influenced by the divine and those where I made choices that ultimately hurt me, when I see how things played out and have come together, I see a divinely guided human experience. I see myself being led to my soul purpose, to my soul's growth, to the lessons I signed up for in this life, to the soul contracts I came here to fulfill, to healing, and ultimately back to God.

The divine is the support system to guide us through the lessons here in this life.

To be clear, I'm not talking about belief. You can believe wholeheartedly and still be disconnected, and you can spend a lifetime going between states of connection and disconnection, as I have. Alternatively, a lack of belief doesn't make the divine go away or cease to have influence in your life. I'm also not saying trauma isn't part of this divine orchestration. What I've come to understand from my own experience is that trauma simply prevents us from connecting deeply with ourselves and with God.

Trauma, big or small, disconnects us from our truth, the truth of who we really are. It's what inhibits us from connecting to spirit, to the divine, to God. It inhibits our intuition and cuts us off from our gifts. It leaves us guessing, seeking, experimenting, trying, convincing ourselves, questioning ourselves, and ultimately unable to trust ourselves, others, or God.

On a physical level, trauma causes our bodies to communicate things to us that may not be true in the present moment. If you try to connect to your intuition, to God, to divine source energy, and trauma is present, your nervous system will block or confuse the communication.

Spiritual people love to tell you to "listen to your body!" You may say, "oh my body is giving me a no," but in reality, your trauma and your nervous system are saying no, and you can't feel anything beyond that. If you have unresolved trauma, stuck emotions, and your nervous system is unable to complete its trauma response cycle, you cannot simply "listen to your body" in any way other than to heal your trauma and nervous system.

Trauma can also block us from connecting with God because we don't believe we're worthy of God's love. If our trauma is rooted in our childhood, as much of it often is, and we have a limiting core belief that we are not worthy of our desires, of joy, of unconditional love, then we will subconsciously block ourselves from those things, which come from God. We simply won't be open to it. So, trauma works on multiple levels to keep us disconnected.

I've often had a distrust for my intuition, which I thought was supposed to come through the body. But when my intuition tried to speak to me through my body, I thought it was just fear, or trauma, ironically. My intuition would tell me someone was cheating or lying, and instead of trusting it, because hello trauma, mother wounds, and my wounded inner child, I told myself I was crazy because that connection was important, and I wanted to be a better person and not let my fear of the past ruin the present. I also questioned why I should trust my intuition or God when I thought at the time that if God had my back, or my intuition wasn't total sh*t, I wouldn't be in that relationship to begin with!

So, you can see the vicious cycle I was perpetuating with my human logic, trauma, and clear disconnection from the divine support that has been with me through it all. This cycle of intuition and trauma and negative outcomes kept affirming my limiting beliefs that my trauma created. Listening to my intuition rarely worked out, and I was affirmed I couldn't trust myself.

Instead of communicating with me via intuition in my body, the divine has communicated with me via intuition in my thoughts, or claircognizance. I simply know things without explanation. Before healing my nervous system, there wasn't ever a feeling in my body or gut, because I was disconnected from my body. I've come to trust divine wisdom in this way, through the mind, because it has often proven itself, it's clear, and hard to argue.

For example, I've always known from when I was a small child that I'd be my own boss when I grew up. I had no clue what I'd be doing, but I knew I wouldn't have a 9-5 office job with a boss to answer to, that's for sure. I also always knew I'd be a mom, and that when it happened it wouldn't be planned, but no matter what the circumstances were when it happened it was the right person at the right time. These were simple truths that followed me my entire life that I didn't question, and they've proven to be pivotal aspects of my journey and soul purpose.

I also have found myself often saying things, giving guidance, or knowing outcomes before they happened, and when asked how I knew, my response would be, "I don't know how, I just know." This has been a common phrase in my life.

I could connect intuitively with my mind but not my body, and as I began to trust this divine wisdom, I began to experiment and heal the trauma in my body and connect that way too.

Now, here's the thing, every moment from that point where I made a choice that I thought was from my intuition, all I had done was hand over the reins to my wounded inner child. This phase of my experience was wrought with chaos, pain, and compounding trauma. However, I recognize how vital each piece of my journey has been. Some of it was my soul, some of it was soul contracts, and a lot of it was trauma. In the greater picture it was all part of my path, each piece played a pivotal role in guiding me to healing, to the mother spirit, to the divine, to God, and now I'm able to teach people about how trauma can inhibit intuition and the connection to the divine and guide them back home.

For example, I had a traumatic breakup with an ex who played a huge role in my spiritual awareness, consciousness, and growth, someone whom I'm still dear friends with today and have the utmost respect for. In the trauma of it all blowing up I decided to move across the country with someone else I barely knew and claimed it as "following my joy." Well, I wasn't even through the Rockies when the joy vanished, and if I had been connected to myself, my truth, my body, and God, I would have gone off on an adventure of my own before heading home.

However, the lessons that were to come were necessary, soul contracts needed to be fulfilled, and so my trauma ensued, I continued on, and within a couple weeks I was pregnant with my son who is quite literally the catalyst for my healing and the work I do with the mother energy for my clients and community.

As someone who has worked with mothers and the mother energy for all of my adult life, I find it fitting that my transition into motherhood was utterly traumatic. At the time I found it unfair, and in the midst of it all I really couldn't understand why I was experiencing so much chaos, fear, pain, and trauma. But it truly was fitting, as it led me deeper into the divine mother than I could have ever gone without it.

If you've read my previous chapters in the She Speaks book series, you'll know a little about my personal journey, but if you haven't, I'll summarize it here with a few more details for context.

I'm a single mom raising my son with the support of my parents in my childhood home. I planned to give birth at home with the support of a midwife and doula, but after twenty hours of effective pushing, I delivered via cesarean with only my son's father present. I wasn't the first person to hold my baby, or the second, or even third. I had to listen to his screams far too long as my heart broke into a million pieces and my guts were open on the table, I was at my lowest in terms of personal power when I became a mother.

I then attempted to navigate some sort of coparenting relationship, which is giving far too much credit with that word choice, while recovering that resulted in my son's father leaving the state after only a week and a half, never to return. The fear of the threats to take my son remained, however, and anxieties from the pandemic that hit four weeks after giving birth, combined with the inherent struggles of recovery and being a single parent prolonged the process and made it that much more difficult. It took me a year to come out of a fog and find the energy to take my healing and the legal journey of establishing custody, visitation, and child support head on.

To say it bluntly, I was a mess. But again, every bit of it was necessary and brought me face to face with the wounds of my inner child that had been holding me back for many years. I was ready for more, for better, for peace.

Instead of blindly experimenting with listening to my body and calling it intuition, I decided to try a healing process of listening to my body through a trauma conscious lens instead. I began to meet myself where I was at, rather than forcing myself to where I wanted to be, being let down, and perpetuating the cycle of distrust. I started to understand what my body was telling me, that it was stressed, tired, scared, and hurt. I began to recognize what my trauma response looked like, what it felt like, and connect with my inner child who was living perpetually in an anxious state.

Slowly, a distinction between my intuition and my trauma response emerged. I was appreciating myself in beautiful new ways, healing on profoundly deep levels, and caring for myself very differently. I was working with the mother energy, like I've done for all of my adult life, but I was finally actually embodying it. The way I nourished and honored myself transformed as I fully integrated the divine mother into my being.

There were some major shifts I witnessed in myself throughout this process. I spent a lot more time with my son, connecting, playing, and being present, because that's what my inner child wanted and needed. I stopped giving in on my boundaries and fully committed to my self-care practices, and I began to recognize quickly when I was needing to delve a bit deeper into self-care and spend some extra time alone. I found myself getting triggered way less in general but in parenting especially my capacity to hold space for tantrums, meltdowns, and tough moments expanded immensely.

I began to recognize that no matter what had ever happened in my life, even when I was jobless, unable to work, or blew up my business, I was always provided for. Somehow, some way, I was never left hanging, on the streets, or hungry. I finally found myself grounded enough and with a great enough capacity to release the chase for money, to surrender my anxiety and fears around it, and the immense pressure I had imposed on myself to create it, and to soften into that trust that I will always be provided for and divinely held.

As I healed my trauma, my nervous system emerged from its perpetual trauma response cycle, and I was able to see my life clearly and finally put full trust in God.

Good thing too, because once I came out of that trauma response and my nervous system was able to finally rest, I could not get enough rest. There was no way I was hustling and grinding with the amount of energy I had and rest I was requiring. At one point I feared that the only way I had ever gotten anything done previously was because of the energy my trauma provided and I wondered if I'd ever have energy again. Luckily, it returned quickly, and with a flood of divine creative energy along with it.

Healing trauma is intense, profound, deep energetic work, and when your nervous system can finally complete its cycle it can rest and digest and you will likely experience a period of deep fatigue. But it's nothing that tons of self-care, fun, and rest can't help, and all of it is part of the beautiful divine process.

For the first time in my life, I was able to tap into unconditional love and truly meet God. I came to see how divine guidance plays a role in both trauma and intuition, and how God never really left me, my trauma simply caused a disconnection. In the short time since, my intuition and divine connection have already deepened and grown exponentially, and I am so grateful.

~ Divinity Speaking ~
"All that stands between you and God is your trauma."

ABOUT THE AUTHOR
HEATHER ROBINSON

Heather Robinson is a guide for conscious re-parenting, inner child healing, and mother wound healing. She is a mentor for women and mothers to expand in all aspects of life by teaching them how to cultivate an inner mother that embodies the spirit and unconditional love of the divine mother. By prioritizing sacred self-care, embodiment, and conscious awareness, Heather empowers women with the tools they need to transform their limiting core beliefs and consistently show up for themselves with love. The integration of the divine mother supports women in evolving beyond the ancestral wounds and harmful family patterns and cycles that hold them back from their goals. Her mission is to help women take their power back, reclaim their fierceness, become wildly confident and anchored in their truth, and access the unconditional love and freedom they've always desired by re-parenting their inner child and consciously choosing a different way.

Website: www.iamhro.com

13
THE AWAKENING

HOLLY BUHLER

There I was, twenty nine and barely surviving. I was a mother of three young children with a husband who traveled a lot and was dealing with severe anxiety and depression.

Things had gotten so bad I could barely leave my house. Every morning I would get my kids ready for school, load them up in the car, drive-thru somewhere to get them breakfast, then let them get out of the car at the school drop-off line.

When school was done, I'd pick them up in the car-pick up line, drive-thru somewhere to get dinner, then head back to our house only to repeat this pattern the next day.

Was it childhood trauma? Was I just sensitive? Was I just crazy? These were the thoughts always swirling around in my head.

I would deal with this pattern for a couple years until finally, my physical health had gotten just as challenging. A bout with "chronic unexplainable hives" would send me on a deep healing journey.

On that journey I had discovered a lot. I learn about how our emotions are actually chemical responses in the body, how those chemicals and other traumas can actually get trapped in the body if not processed correctly. I also learned about Highly Sensitive People and Empaths.

One of the most profound realizations in my personal journey was realizing I was both a Highly Sensitive Person, Emotional Empath, and Physical Empath.

Not only was I highly attuned to the subtle changes & nuances with people and environments, the emotional and physical empathic abilities in me would feel or take on other people's emotions and physical ailments *as if they were my own.*

While much of the anxiety and depression symptoms I had experienced could be explained by childhood trauma, the severity of the symptoms was truly explained by having these abilities. The traumas would naturally affect me deeply. Perhaps more deeply than the average person without these abilities.

For much of my life, I would experience these things but have absolutely no idea what was going on. I didn't know why going to my child's school classroom filled with all the other parents made me want to cry and run for the exit. I didn't know why I just couldn't bring myself to sit in my church service room and sat in the empty hall instead. I didn't know why I was always bombarded with negative and insecure thoughts when around others.

Being alone was my only haven, or with a few sacred people who actually felt comforting to me.

While some would call these curses, I now choose to call them abilities. I didn't always feel this way. I used to hate them.

There was a transition period between gaining awareness of what was going on, to finally figuring out how to manage these abilities. In the beginning stages of awareness, I still found myself in a victim state. A large portion of the anxiety and depression dissipated simply with the question, "Is this mine?"

However, it wasn't the full solution. I knew what was mechanically happening, but still felt powerless to the situation. Walking into a room and feeling sad, angry, afraid for 'seemingly no reason' was exhausting.

In this period of time, I still found myself avoiding group gatherings. But it was then because I was choosing to stay away out of awareness of simply not wanting the experience. I didn't want my mental, emotional, and physical states to be at the whim of the people I happened to be around at any given moment.

I would avoid certain people or places under the excuse of, "I don't want to be around them because I can feel how they feel towards me, and I can hear what they think of me." There were many family gatherings or events that I chose not to attend for these reasons as well.

While I was in awareness, I still wasn't in empowerment.

I knew this couldn't last forever though. I wanted to find a way to live a fulfilling life while not avoiding so much; not allow others and their own poor internal states influence my life choices.

THE ALIGNMENT

I knew there had to be another way. After learning about my intuitive and empathic abilities I started working as an Intuitive Energy Practitioner. As I worked with clients and found the roots of their mental and emotional patterns, I learned about myself along the way. I learned that while I was in fact an emotional empath, the extent of what I was experiencing didn't have to be.

The more I healed my subconscious conditioning and cleaned up my energy fields, the less intense the mechanics of being an Empath felt. I was able to feel the emotions and let them flow through me rather than absorb them.

I realized that I had patterns of avoidance that created a lot of resentment. While I often spoke up for the victim or underdog, when it was me that needed speaking up for, I would stay silent. Many times, the energy would build over long periods of time until the situation became so large, I could no longer handle it. By that time, people had become so accustomed to me not saying anything, when I did actually speak up, it wasn't received well.

The avoidance stemming from not wanting to feel the emotional upset or turmoil of the other person. It was easier to go along with the flow rather than say no and then FEEL just how annoyed or angry someone was with me. It was easier to hide and not shine in my work rather than feel the insecurities it may have brought up in others. The avoidance came from a genuine desire to not be the perceived 'cause' of the other, but it was also slightly selfish. I didn't want to feel their stuff.

Taking on excessive amounts of responsibility for others' emotional states is a classic pattern that emotional empaths experience. At a young age we put two and two together, that "when I do (fill in the blank) action, so-and-so feels (fill in the blank emotion)" and we come to the incorrect conclusion that, "that must be my fault."

In this period of self-discovery, I learned that I had done a LOT of adapting and changing who I was to fit what others wanted since childhood. I had completely lost who I was along the way.

The path of personal alignment was both a shedding of what wasn't me... and also a discovery of what actually was.

THE SHELL

Over time, it was as if I had a shell of plaster trapping the real me inside. Each time betraying myself by saying yes when I truly wanted to say no... saying no when I truly wanted to say yes, more and more plaster being slapped over the top of me.

Each time I didn't speak or share things for fear of hearing someone's mind chatter and interpret it as rejection. Changing how I expressed (or didn't) express myself and changing what I looked like.

While on the outside my 'statue' of plaster may have looked happy or beautiful, it wasn't the real me. It was the version of me I thought the world wanted. How impossible a task that was because not a single person would agree on what the perfect person was like!

These moments of sickness and emotional distress had created 'cracks' in the plaster. It was easy to judge these moments. To view them as wrong or too painful. Really, these were gifts from the Universe. These moments that seemed to break me were what allowed me to dig deep and search within. To no longer live on the surface.

The real me was trying desperately to get out. My soul wanted to grow and expand. It wanted to evolve... but as long as I was trapped behind the facade of the fake image of plaster... I couldn't.

As I started to embrace the cracks, I saw a beautiful glistening underneath. A version of me that was strong yet gentle, fierce yet kind, honest and merciful. Piece by piece I was able to shed the layers of lies I had been telling myself.

Lies like: Be quiet. Don't be too loud. Don't share your opinions. Don't ask for too much. Don't annoy people. Don't be a burden to others. You're not enough. No one wants what you have to offer. (And so much more)

This process of shedding the shell of lies wasn't easy. There were intense periods of time where I wasn't sure if the potential, I saw underneath the shells was actually me or not. I found myself still searching out all the personality systems, astrology, and human design systems in an effort to find out who I truly was.

Shedding a false foundation to rebuild one in truth can be very destabilizing. In the path of self-discovery, I found myself and others going from giving away our power and self-identity to others to then systems, and neither was true. One day I realized, what I was searching for wasn't a moment of pure self-discovery of a complete person based on a chart or system.

"Who I truly am and who I get to be, is actually a mix of my true essence on a soul level AND who I CHOOSE to become."

— HOLLY BUHLER

The pieces of plaster are still shedding, and the beautiful soul underneath it is still evolving. The thing that keeps me steadfast in the journey is my intuition. Giving myself permission to be guided and led by my gut and my heart vs getting up in my head and trying to figure it all out of what others want.

SHINE

In my coaching I do a lot of life mission and purpose work. I have an ability to tune in to the essence of a person on a soul level. To see through the plaster and get to what's underneath.

While many come to me searching for their 'mission & purpose' I find it important to distinguish how I view these two things separately.

I believe *our PURPOSE is to be the best version of our true selves that we can be.* If we were to do nothing else in this life but be our true selves, we would have served our purpose beautifully.

Our MISSION is a task we set to accomplish via living out our purpose. Some have missions that seem to reach larger numbers of people, and some have missions that seem to reach smaller numbers. Neither is better or worse. We need all of them. There is no ability to measure the ripple effect one person can have on the world by living their divinity daily.

It's also important to realize, the best version of us isn't the perfect one. It isn't the most elevated one who never makes mistakes. It's the version of us that's genuinely trying. That has personal awareness of our own triggers. That does our best to take personal accountability when needed. That's willing to apologize. That's willing to forgive. That also holds healthy internal and external boundaries.

When our divinity speaks is when we truly shine.

Our divinity speaks in the moments we listen to our hearts and share the authentic parts of ourselves.

What used to bring me so much pain, now fuels my work as an intuitive energy practitioner and coach. That mind chatter I used to hear anytime I was around others, I now harness during sessions. Guiding me to know EXACTLY where my clients are stuck, in fear, or feeling insecure.

That gift of being an emotional empath, now helps me to know exactly what emotions my clients are experiencing, even when they can't even identify them on their own.

The same gifts and abilities that once brought me so much pain now bring joy and success to my own life as well as others. I didn't need to change who I was; I just needed to learn how to truly love and accept myself and harness my light for good.

GUIDED IMAGERY

Imagine you're on a beautiful beach with crystal clear blue waters. As you walk down the beach you feel the soft white sand beneath your toes. You smell a mix of coconut and salt water in the air. You feel the warmth of the sunshine on your skin as a gentle breeze cools you off.

As you walk down the beach you realize you don't have a voice. A few meters down the shoreline you see an iridescent shine in the sand. As you walk towards it you see a beautiful shell. As you approach you bend down to pick it up. You grab the soft shell in one hand and brush the sand off of it in the other. As you do so you see that your name is etched into the shell. In an instant a memory flashes before your eyes.

The sea-witch took your voice because you thought it was the only way for you to get what you wanted. You realize inside this shell is your true voice.

A representation of everything you could ever be, everything you would ever want, and everything you'll ever want to become.

The world had convinced you that you couldn't have it all. That you couldn't be YOU...

... AND be happy

... AND be successful

... AND be wealthy

... AND have friendships

... AND have good relationships

But you see now that it was all a lie.

You see that the way to truly be happy, have fulfilling success, have thriving friendships and relationships is actually to be YOU... all of you. That there is grace and mercy for you. There is a place for you. And the world NEEDS you.

As you have this realization you see the shell crumble in your hands and disintegrate. Leaving only a glowing light in its place. You scoop this glowing light into your hands and gently yet powerfully bring it into your heart space leaving the palms of your hands resting on your chest.

This authentic voice travels from your heart up into your 5th chakra in your throat. From now on, everything you say and do will filter through your heart first. As this light rests in your throat, you feel a warmth in your heart up to your throat. It's a burning desire to share your light and divinity with the world and a deep connection to sharing who you truly are.

Sit with this visualization for a moment and ask what your heart wants to share with the world today.

~ Divinity Speaking ~
"Your purpose is more important than you could ever know. You are needed!"

ABOUT THE AUTHOR

HOLLY BUHLER

Holly Buhler is a Soul-Aligned Success Coach and founder of The Confidence Academy. She helps purpose-driven women create soul & energy aligned businesses that are fulfilling & sustainable; while maintaining thriving personal lives. To create this transformation, Holly blends her skills from over 20 years in the Health & Wellness industry. She also incorporates additional modalities including Human Design, Rapid Transformational Therapy →, NLP/TIME Techniques, Akashic Records, The Life Coach School, and more into her work. After traveling the US in an RV for a year, Holly, her husband, and three of their four children have re-settled near St. Louis, MO.

Website: www.hollybuhler.com

Social Media: @hollybuhlercoach

Free FB Community: Brave Women Rising

14

THE SOUND OF DIVINITY IS
WONDERFULL

JESS HOEPER

I was sitting in the second row pew. I was trying not to cry, as hard as I could, because when I do cry, I cry loud tears. To fight back the tears, I was fidgeting with a bracelet I had received the day before. The bracelet spelled out HOPE, four cubes each with a letter.

The day before I had been shopping for funeral clothes. I had just months prior had my second child and nothing fit quite right. When I went to purchase the clothes, the clerk asked if I wanted to donate money to childhood cancer research, in return I would get a bracelet. I was shopping for funeral clothes for my grandfather, he was one of the most giving men I have ever known. In this moment, I said yes in his honor without hesitation!

While sitting in the second row, listening to the pastor talk about how "Ray helped other people everyday", I was spinning the cubes on the bracelet. In that moment time slowed down and I heard the *wonderFULL* and familiar voice of the Divine putting the pieces together. "**H** is Help, **O** is Other, **P** is People and **E** is Everyday." Hope is made active by helping other people everyday. My life's mission was set and etched onto my heart. This would fuel my soul's mission then and to this day.

This was the loudest GOD wink moment to date. I have had many more Divine conversations and remember many from my lifetime, but this was a BIG one, so loud you couldn't miss it. Fitting for me, it was in a church. I grew up going to church. I loved the collectiveness of prayer in church. Being with others praying and around others praying felt electric. The power of collective prayer is electric!

After this God wink moment, I would start my own business called: Ray of HOPE, LLC. Ray is my grandfather's name and HOPE was the message. I get to honor this Divine message on a daily basis! My business focuses on building reflective practice, enhancing self+awareness, and helping the helpers within the human service world. I am a social worker by training and have spent much of my career in the world of child welfare. Through my social work journey, I found the power of reflection. Reflection can help us notice the messages or conversations with the Divine we had and hadn't quite internalized or digested.

My business is built around the idea of *active hope.* Hope to me is made active by **H**elping **O**ther **P**eople **E**veryday. My current role as business owner and reflective coach has afforded me the opportunity to work in a divinely connected way, while still working with systems that are struggling.

Divinity is uniquely speaking to us all, albeit sometimes very loudly, and other times through a whispering wind. We need to tap into all of our senses to take it in and connect. What does Divinity sound like? What does Divinity feel like? What does Divinity look like? What does Divinity smell/taste like? No comparisons needed; how does Divinity speak to you uniquely?

THE *WONDERFULL* SOUND OF DIVINITY

I most strongly connect with Divinity through hearing; the sounds I hear or the messages I hear internally. I have heard and put to work the voice of the Divine in my personal and professional life. The thing that all of these moments of 'hearing' have in common is that they are deeply intimate and heard by me uniquely. Even in the church moment, when my HOPE message came, where external happenings put into place my internal integration of my soul's mission, no one was with me in that moment, receiving the message, other than the Divine!

Every time I connect with the Divine through hearing, I am left in a state of Awe and Wonder! Those feelings are part of how I know it was Divine communication. Divinity for me has always been a *WONDER filled* experience, making Divinity WonderFULL to me! Divinity speaking never brings out the judgmental sides of us, in fact it opens up wonder and curiosity. Divine wants to connect and mend that which is disconnected.

I remember as a young adult, hearing a Divine message that said "You will have five children", I did not take this too seriously. I did tell my roommate at the time that "I think I will have five kids." She responded with "Do you want five kids?" To which I said "Yeah I think so". This message briefly left me in a deep state of wonder, how could this possibly be? I had not met my husband at this point in my life, so I let this message go and would not remember it again until I did have 5 kids! When my fifth and final child was born, my old roommate messaged me saying, "You really did know you were going to have five kids." And then I remembered the moment I received that message. I knew that it was Divinity speaking to me, but in young adulthood, I was not in a deep relationship with the Divine, where we work together, like I am at this point in my life. It was a beautiful full circle moment that reminded me that Divinity had been speaking to me through messages of sound for a long time.

The sound of Divinity is pure LOVE, unconditional love. Even if you are receiving redirection messages, they are loving and safe. The Divine is not out to harm you ever, only to lovingly guide you and support you!

A major way the Divine connects with me through sound messages now is often also connected with vision, through names or a picture flash. Have you ever heard in your mind or in your heart, the name of a person or friend? Or have you seen their face come to mind and you aren't always sure why or how come? Well, this is what I call "FRIENDTUITION" and "CONNECTUITION". This is Divinity speaking to you, asking you to connect with a friend, or sometimes someone completely unknown! I used to see a friend's face or hear their name strongly in my mind or heart, and sometimes I would reach out or often I would ignore it. I was a little confused about why they were so loudly in my awareness. Over time I have grown in understanding and faith in the Divine, that friends or even complete strangers are loudly on my mind or heart, so that I connect with them. I don't need to understand the 'why' as that will often reveal itself with time. And even if the 'why' doesn't appear, a love-filled connection is never a waste of time. Over time I have comfortably accepted that this has been a Divine direction to reach out to that person and pray for them. Pray that they are healthy, well and aligned. Never has it been coincidental that they show up in my mind or heart. This is Divinity speaking to me.

THE *WONDERFULL* TOUCH OF DIVINITY

Reflecting on how we feel (through touch) Divinity, brought up so many moments of pure joy. I am the mother of five kids and each time a new baby was placed into my arms, I remember feeling overwhelmed with joy and connection to the Divine, through touch, their soft squishy skin, their fine hair, and their tiny little body. These moments are Divine just to think about.

The outdoors/nature is where I can 'feel' (through touch) Divinity on a grand scale and very readily. The flowers, trees, in the wind, through the visuals, etc. I can feel the interconnection of Divinity when I am in nature, the energy of interconnection is palpable! Have you ever stood amongst a group of cosmos flowers? They are tall and wispy with flowers at the very tip top. The wispy stems are soft and there is an ease to running your hands through them. This feeling is as electric as the feeling of collective prayer for me. Standing amongst the cosmos flowers, grounds me, and makes me feel small, in a connected to the collective way!

THE *WONDERFULL* LOOK OF DIVINITY

The Divine paints the most beautiful pictures for us to connect with and 'see' it in action; through witnessing a couple deeply in love hold hands, or through a sunset that is shining through the clouds shooting out glorious sun rays, or through the soft smile of a stranger that says "we are connected and I love you too". I feel like the wonder filled visuals from the collective is magnificence in the most obvious form.

I also connect with the Divine through visions of light variations, sometimes I will see a face of a person and it will be backlit or brightly lit up. I have had experiences of seeing almost a flashing brightness around someone, even complete strangers, this now tells me to connect with that person (the CONNECTUITION I talked about earlier).

THE *WONDERFULL* SMELL OF DIVINITY

Hear me out, I know this sounds odd on the surface, but I have thought a lot about senses and their relationship to connecting with the Divine.

For me, when I reflected on feeling divinely connected through scent/smell, I thought of fresh cut grass. I live in Minnesota, so grass being mowed only occurs, at most, six months out of the year, but the smell is so refreshing and reminds me of earthly growth and renewal. Connection to Divinity through smell weaves right into my feeling of Divinity. The scent of food is another way Divinity connects me to community, culture, family; the sharing of love through food, you can smell the love in the air! Notice all of the ways Divinity can be sensed through smell.

LISTEN FOR THE *WONDERFULL* SOUND OF DIVINITY

Divinity is speaking to all of us all of the time. My heightened sense that is connected to Divinity is SOUND. How this is experienced by me may be the same or different than how it is experienced by you, but no matter how it is happening, the key is IT IS HAPPENING!! And it meets you right where you are. I can think of times the writings of Lorna Byne, C.S. Lewis or Ram Daas is what found me and connected me closer to the Divine. At other moments it came through nature, other times it came through the voice of a friend, and yet other times it came through the quiet within my own heart.

Through all of our senses, whichever is strongest for you, are the interwoven emotions.   Divinity makes us **FEEL** something. Connecting to Divinity, our souls, and the power of the collective, through our senses, makes us feel alive!!!

Divinity does make us *aware* of disconnection, but only in an effort to gift us the knowingness so we can bridge disconnection with intentional connection, through love.

If 'hearing' Divinity is not how you most strongly connect with the Divine, that is fine, but reflect on how you connect and honor that connection through intentional space and time for it both in business and in life.

So much of Divinity speaking is felt and not seen, that we have to be intentional about sharing our experiences so others become deeply connected to *their* experiences.

$\text{\&}$

DIVINITY CONNECTION REFLECTION:

Because building reflective practices is the mission of the business I have built, I wanted to share a reflective opportunity with you too!

Take the time to get cozy, warm and situated.

Grab a journal.

Ask the Divine to join you in this moment.

Reflect on how you connect with the Divine. Take a minute or two for each of these questions.

What senses are most activated when you feel most connected to the Divine? When you think of your greatest most 'obvious' Godwink moments, how did they come? Did you see the Divine? Did you hear the Divine? Did you feel the Divine? Did you taste/smell the Divine? What emotions were strongest? Love? Connection to collective? Did you hear any mission moving messages within the connection?

End with a prayer of gratitude; *"Thank you Divine team for connecting with me through all of my senses and evoking feelings of love and gratitude, I connect with you with ease and we connect often, I give you love and I receive your love. Amen"*

~ *Divinity Speaking* ~
"The WonderFULL sense of Divinity is around, within and amongst us all, all of the time."

ABOUT THE AUTHOR

JESS HOEPER

Jess Hoeper is a Social Worker, Reflective Coach, Mother, and Founder of Ray of Hope, LLC. Jess works nationally with Human Service Professionals and Leaders, enhancing self-awareness and system-awareness through reflection (reflective coaching). Jess's passion is curating curiosity and spending time in wonder. Jess has recently added international best-selling author to her tagline, as she co-authored the books "Where Social Work Can Lead You" and "Success Codes: Secrets To Success You Weren't Taught In School." She also participates in column writing and public speaking; her favorite topic is "unconditioning our love for each other". Personally, Jess and her husband are raising their five kids on a farm in central Minnesota.

Website: www.rayofhopereflectivecoaching.com

Instagram: @reflective_coaching

Facebook: Ray of HOPE

Email: jesshoeper@live.com

15

WHICH VOICE ARE YOU LISTENING TO?

JUDIE HURTADO

That's never going to work!

That's not enough!

You need to do more!

You need to work harder!

The Two Voices

Has anyone ever said those things to you? Better yet, have you ever said those things to yourself?

That Voice, which I call The Inner Bully, has ruled most of my life. It has stolen countless moments of joy, success and celebration. Every time I accomplished something, I would hear that it wasn't a big deal or that more clients should have registered or that I could have done more.

The Inner Bully was incessant. It was loud and seemed impossible for me to ignore. Actually, I don't think I even tried to ignore it because I believed it to be true. Well, once in a while I would talk back to it. I would argue and provide reasons why I was successful or that what I had accomplished was good enough. I even started making lists as evidence to prove that the Inner Bully was wrong. While making lists did help somewhat, the Inner Bully didn't seem to care. It always returned with something to say that made me feel bad about myself. No matter what I did, it was never satisfied with me, my actions or my accomplishments.

At the same time, I was also aware of another Voice. This Voice was totally different. It was softer. Gentler. It felt peaceful and calm. This Voice did not make me feel like a failure or that I wasn't good enough. This Voice would offer me short but sweet answers when I connected with it.

For example, this Voice said things like:

The answers will be revealed (when I asked about a problem).

Not yet.

Rest.

Be patient.

Yes!

No.

I find it a little challenging to give this Voice a specific name because it's truly so many things. It's my Soul, my Inner Wise Self, my Higher Self, and my Intuition. This Voice quietly whispered that my husband was 'the one' when we first met over 23 years ago. This Voice said "No" when I was considering a business training program. (By the way, I didn't listen at first!)

The crazy thing is that even though I was aware of these two Voices and I knew that listening to one made me feel good and listening to the other one made me feel bad, I still continued to listen to the Inner Bully more often than not. It was always the louder one. It was comforting and familiar, as strange as that may sound. The Inner Bully made sense to me because it reflected back my own fears and beliefs.

THE SHIFT

Even though I was able to see, hear and know things ever since I could remember, as a child and young woman, I didn't think I had any intuitive gifts. I never fathomed that I would become a Spiritual Teacher, although my interest in spiritual things, like crystals and tarot cards, began at a young age.

I graduated from Syracuse University with a dual degree in Magazine Journalism and International Relations. From there, I worked in Corporate America in Advertising and Magazine Publishing. All the while, the Inner Bully was always forcing me to work harder and to do more. My Soul was also speaking to me but... I just wasn't as connected or aware.

Eventually, things began to transform as my life shifted. I got married, left Corporate America and became a mother. When my daughters were in preschool, I followed my passions and became a Health and Wellness writer and a Certified Yoga Teacher. I received my first Reiki Level I attunement in 2009, studied with various teachers and became a Reiki Master in 2011. As I dove deeper and deeper into my spiritual practices, my Inner Bully remained quite active but my Soul started to get louder as well. The more I listened and followed my Soul's Voice, the more fulfilled and happier I became. Plus, my intuitive gifts began to explode.

My Soul encouraged me to start sharing my gifts with my community. As I studied to become a Reiki Master, I began facilitating healing sessions to my friends. My friends were amazed at the information I channeled and the sensations they were experiencing during their sessions with me. They were the ones who pushed me to start a spiritual business.

FYI, sometimes your Soul communicates to you through other people!

KNOW THIS

Everyone has a Soul and a Soul's Voice (or Higher Self, Intuition, Inner Knowing, whatever you decide to call it, you have it). You may not be aware of it but it's there. Once you set the intention to hear, feel, sense or just know, you will connect with your Soul. It really can be that simple.

You have been conditioned to pay attention to the Inner Bully and, likely, many other Voices that have not served you or no longer serve you. Know that you have the power and the capability to distinguish these Voices and decide which one to listen to.

Many of my clients have asked me if I actually hear a Voice. Most times I do hear a Voice, although it's an internal voice. Other times the Voice communicates to me through a feeling, a knowing, or a vision. Sometimes my Soul gives me a message through an oracle card, something I read on social media, a song on the radio or a conversation I overheard while waiting in line at the grocery store. It's different for everyone. Trust that you will know how your Soul wants to communicate with you. It already has been communicating with you.

CREATING THE IDEAL CONDITIONS

There is no wrong or right way to connect with your Soul. You don't need to light a candle or burn incense, although those tools may be fun and helpful.

One important ingredient is Silence. In my experience, my Soul's Voice tends to be on the quieter side. There's so much noise in the world and in our minds. Cultivating silence helps with everything.

Rumi said it best, "Silence gives answers."

SOUL & INTUITION ACTIVATION:

I created this Activation to support you in connecting with your Soul and intuition. This Activation is infused with my unique blend of Reiki and various forms of Healing Energy. This Activation comes from the highest and most aligned healing energy and frequency.

By reading and practicing this Activation, you will amplify your Intuition and connection to your Soul to the highest degree that you are ready for at this time.

This Activation is simple. There is no need for you to work hard or force anything. No effort is involved, just your intention and desire.

Let's begin.

1. Find a comfortable seated position. Ideally you will be in a quiet area where you will not be disturbed.
2. Create a Sacred Intention. One example may be: *It is my Sacred Intention to Activate and Strengthen my Intuition* or *I am connected with my Soul*. Or *I clearly hear my Intuition*. Come up with one that resonates with you. You can speak it out loud and/or write it down.
3. Close your eyes.

4. Bring your attention to your breath. Focus on the rise and fall of your breath while taking 5 deep inhalations and exhalations.

5. Find an area inside your body where you feel, sense or know it holds the energy of your Sacred Intention. It may be your heart, your belly, your womb or another area of your body. Trust whatever comes through.

6. If it feels comfortable and available to you, place your hands on that part of your body. Continue to breathe deeply.

7. When you feel ready, ask a question. Start with something simple such as *What do you want me to know today?* Or *Can you give me a word or a symbol or image?* Be open and curious. You may suddenly hear, know or see the message. If nothing comes through, that's ok. Trust that you have started the process to connect with your Soul and Intuition. You may receive a message later, while taking a walk, in the shower, journaling, or making dinner.

8. Whenever you feel complete, give thanks.

9. Open your eyes, move, stretch and drink some water. You may wish to journal and write down whatever information you received and any thoughts you have about what you experienced. Writing it down can cement your experience. The Inner Bully wants you to forget.

10. Ideally, you will practice this every day. Like with most things, the more you do it, the easier it becomes. After time, you will develop a strong, close relationship with your Soul and that Voice, however it communicates with you, will grow.

❦

Moving Forward:

Congratulations! You have begun a new relationship with your Soul and your Soul's Voice. Remember that connection will look and feel differently for everyone. It will likely change and evolve over time. Trust the process and the unfolding. This relationship is the most important one you will ever have.

~ Divinity Speaking ~
"All the questions that you ask and all the guidance that you seek can be found within. Ask, Listen and Receive."

ABOUT THE AUTHOR

JUDIE HURTADO

Judie Hurtado is a healer and spiritual teacher with nearly 40 years of personal and professional experience. She has received extensive trainings and certifications in various healing modalities such as Subconscious Mind Transformation and is a Certified Intuitive Counselor and Certified Ordained Minister.

Judie is also a Reiki Master and infuses all of her work with this incredible healing energy. As a Kali Bruja and Priestess, she helps women connect to their own powerful intuition so that they make wise choices to create a life they truly love. She has supported thousands of clients online and in person through Intuitive Guidance sessions, Moon Blessings, Group Portals and Oracle Card readings. She has been featured on numerous podcasts including The Gathering Movement and highlighted in hipnewjersey.com.

Judie, a native New Yorker, lives in Maplewood, New Jersey with her husband Marco, daughters Sofia and Alessandra and their sweet rescue dog, Mama.

Website: www.judiehurtado.com/

Instagram:@judiehurtadointuitive

Facebook Group: Magic, Miracles and Manifestations with Judie Hurtado

THE RICHNESS OF LIFE, WHEN I LISTEN TO MY HEART

JULIE AIRD

*L*istening to my heart is something I always knew how to do, in fact we all do. It comes to us naturally when we are children. But as we grow up, we learn ways to adjust and fit in, ways to become more acceptable to our families and communities. And in order to do this, we often stop listening to our hearts. Our heads become the driving force in our lives.

But I've learned that by listening and following my heart I experience the most fulfillment, satisfaction and meaning life has to offer. Sometimes it has meant leaving relationships or jobs, or letting go of the things my head told me were the safe and secure things to do, but were also leaving my soul feeling empty. Listening to my heart has involved risk. And sometimes it has meant loss, as I've let go of one way of living and embraced another. But when I look back over my life, I see that the richest experiences I've had were when I listened to my heart and followed it. So, I make a conscious choice to live from my heart on a daily basis. It's an ever-evolving practice.

I believe that the heart is where our true self lives and that it is also our connection to the Divine. When we listen to it, it speaks loving messages to us, and it invites us to expand, so that we don't stay limited, confined to the life our head wants us to live. Living from our hearts is where the most profound experiences of love, peace, passion, freedom, grace and fulfillment happen.

I had a lot of dating experiences with different guys in my teens and early twenties. When I was twenty-three, I met a special guy on a weekend ski trip. We really connected because of our similar spiritual beliefs. As soon as the weekend ended, we started dating, and it didn't take long before we fell in love. We spent all of our time together outside of work, and became very dependent on each other. We didn't have many outside activities. I didn't realize at the time that this was unhealthy, I just knew I really loved him and enjoyed spending time with him.

After a year of dating, we started talking about getting married. It was summer, and I was working part-time at a dinner theater in the evenings after work. One night after rehearsal, he came to pick me up and suggested we stay for the show. I thought that seemed kind of odd. I wasn't performing that night so I was free to stay, but as one of their employees, I didn't really care to watch the show. I was only there to rehearse that day, plus, I was wearing my dance clothes, and didn't have anything to change into. But he insisted we stay, so I borrowed a dress and shoes from a fellow coworker backstage, and met him in the dining room.

During the show, there was a time when the performers would acknowledge anniversaries and birthdays in the audience. When they invited those who were celebrating to stand, I saw my boyfriend leave the table and walk right up on stage. I thought, "What is he doing?" That was so unlike him as he didn't like being in front of people. But then he called me up on stage, and in front of the entire audience, got down on one knee and asked me to marry him! He had the ring and everything! I was so shocked as it was unexpected. We had talked about getting engaged in another six months or so, but not now! I remember being in the women's restroom later that evening, and some ladies asked me if I knew he was going to ask me. I told them I had no idea.

I was excited to get engaged, but when I reflected back on that night, I realized I felt some pressure to say "yes" because we were in front of all those people. How could I turn him down on stage? I mean, I did love him, and was planning to say "yes" to him at some point, but I felt it was too soon. His reason for rushing was because his best friend who lived out of the country would be visiting in a few months, and he wanted him to be the best man.

So we proceeded to plan our wedding, setting the date, and securing the venue...and then I started to have some doubts. I wasn't sure where these doubts were coming from because I hadn't had *any* when I was dating him. At first, I thought maybe I was just afraid to get married. My parents had divorced a year earlier, and I thought I was having cold feet about marriage in general. But as the weeks progressed, I realized that it was *him* that I was afraid of marrying. And after a few months of continuing to have doubts, I began to see he was not the best fit for me.

I remember visualizing our lives in the future, and I just saw us going down different paths. I knew I was going to be expanding as a person, and he had very set ideas about how to do things, and how he wanted to do life. I was afraid he wasn't going to support me in the things I wanted to do in the future. But I was also afraid of breaking up with him because it would be such a huge loss. The idea of not being with him felt like I was staring at a big black hole, and I couldn't see anything beyond that.

Even though I knew breaking up would mean pain and facing the unknown, I couldn't get over the feeling that this was not right, so I trusted my heart and ended the relationship. I was devastated and I felt like I was starting my life over. I had given up many of my friends when we dated, so I was really lonely. A couple of months later, a college friend called me and invited me to a singles group. I felt a sense of embarrassment about having a broken engagement, but I went anyway. That group was such a support. It gave me a whole new circle of friends.

A couple of years later, at one of our group events, I met a wonderful man. It was a boat cruise and dinner party, and after we met, we talked most of the evening. I felt so comfortable with him. We connected over many things, including both having ended serious relationships a couple of years prior. We had each learned so much from those breakups, and were consciously choosing to change the codependent patterns we had in those relationships. Now we were looking for someone with whom we could maintain our individuality, while still experiencing love and support in the relationship. It was like we were two whole people coming together.

After that night, I was so excited about meeting someone I felt so aligned with. I hardly slept for days. But I wasn't sure if I'd see him again, since he wasn't a regular member of our group, and he hadn't asked for my number. So when he called me a few days later to ask me out, I was ecstatic! As soon as we started dating, I knew he was different from any other man I had ever dated. In fact, after my broken engagement, I made a lengthy list of the things I wanted in a partner and this man was checking off every item on my list. I couldn't believe it!

This year we celebrated twenty-six years of marriage. He is my best friend, partner, spiritual companion, and soul mate. He has supported me in everything I ever wanted to do. We've had a beautiful life together, and have been blessed to raise an amazing son. I know that if I hadn't made that decision to listen to my heart and break up with that other man, I would not have had the life I've had. It was the best decision I ever made.

So what do I mean when I say "live from my heart"? And what does it mean to move from my head to my heart? Well, first, a little more about the head. Our head is where we judge ourselves. It's where all the negative messages we tell ourselves come from. It's the part of us that tells us what we 'should' do, and also who we are not. For example, it will say things like... "You're not good enough. You don't matter. You're not worthy."

Our heart is a quieter voice inside us. It's the part of us that speaks messages of love, acceptance and ease. When we listen to it, we are filled with love for ourselves and others, and we want to shine out and be our contribution to the world. Many of us don't realize there are these two parts to us. We are so attached to our heads that we think it *is* us. We think what it is telling us is true. And we don't realize that there is another voice to guide us, another way to live.

It was a profound awakening for me when I realized that there were these two parts of me. There was this head part that would operate on its own, run wild if I let it, and tell me all kinds of negative, fear-based messages. But there was another part of me, speaking much more loving and peaceful messages, and that was my heart.

So I decided to start consciously choosing to listen to my heart. It's really just a practice. A practice of noticing when I am saying things to myself that are coming from that negative headspace, as opposed to listening and connecting to my heart. My heart is what I know now is my connection to Divinity, God, Spirit, Source (whatever word you choose to call it). My heart is the part of me that tells me I'm loved, I'm special, and that I'm here for a divine purpose. And when I'm listening to it, I experience peace, love, joy and enthusiasm towards life. I feel excited and passionate about being on the planet and contributing to the world. My life is richer and much more fulfilling.

When I was a little girl, I loved to ice skate. My family lived in Chicago, and we had an ice rink near our home. I began figure skating at the age of two...actually there wasn't a lot of skating going on then. It was more like marching on ice. But I took lessons for about five years and got increasingly better and had some tricks I'd do. When I was seven, my dad got transferred with his job, and my family made a big move to California. When we did that, my parents told me that I wasn't going to be able to skate anymore because the ice rink was too far away. I was really, really sad about that.

After that, I always felt like there was this unlived dream inside of me. I continued to watch figure skating and idolized skaters like Kristi Yamaguchi and Michelle Quan. I even had the Dorothy Hamill haircut! I always thought if I had kept skating, I could have been like one of them. I love everything about figure skating.... the creativity, the dance movements, the performance aspect, the beauty, the precision. It all fit who I was. And so, growing up, whenever I got the opportunity to skate at birthday parties or with friends, I would do that, but I never took lessons again.

When I turned fifty, my heart was longing to skate again. I decided to buy myself a pair of ice skates for my birthday. They were so pretty, with little diamonds on the shoelaces, and they just sparkled. I loved them and was excited to start skating again. But when I went out on the ice this time, having not skated for years, I was a lot more scared to fall than I ever had been. All the young kids on the ice made me nervous, and I didn't feel comfortable at all. I was so disappointed. Now that I was older, I realized this was not going to be the same experience I had once had. So, I put the skates in the closet and tried to forget about it.

But when I left my full-time job a few years later, I had a lot more time on my hands and was connecting with my heart on a daily basis.

The ice-skating idea came right back. The little kid inside of me really wanted to ice skate. So, I went skating during a midweek morning session, which I hoped would be less crowded. The first person I saw was a woman in her eighties, with a cute little skirt on, skating fearlessly. I thought, if this woman can do it, I can do it! I ended up resuming lessons again, and I had a ball. The little kid inside me was so excited and happy! I even got to meet some US and World Champions that trained at my rink. It was exhilarating to be in that environment again. One thing I've learned is that if the inner child in me is happy, I am most definitely in my heart. All those feelings of enthusiasm, joy, and freedom are our clues. Our inner child knows the way.

❧

In 2019, my heart was calling me into the next chapter of life, that of being a coach, speaker and author. This meant leaving my twenty-year job, and thirty-year career in higher education. It was not an easy decision, leaving the security, the structure, the routine, and the title I had. It felt like a huge risk, knowing that I was now going to need to create my own income. But in spite of all that, I still did it. I had built up enough experiences in life to know that when I listened to my heart and followed, everything worked out.

I remember feeling pretty uncomfortable the first few months after I left. This was the first time in my life I had ever taken a break from either being a student or employee. I became so aware of my need to be productive and perform. I realized that for my whole life I had been driven to find my value through 'doing'. Just 'being' was a foreign concept.

So, when I first left my job and started building my coaching business, I took my pushing and hustling way of doing things into this venture as well. But then I burned out once more. Listening to my heart meant I needed to let go of this way of functioning as well. I had already let go of my thirty-year career, the identities, titles and roles. And now I was letting go of the *way* I was doing my coaching business, the pushing and doing, the performing and the need to be productive. All I was left with was *me*.

I thought I would feel a big hole inside myself, but surprisingly, I didn't feel that way. I began to really enjoy spending time by myself, being quiet, and just 'being'. I had always tried to find fulfillment outside of myself, but now I realized there was nothing I needed to add to myself to be fulfilled. Even my fears about money began to slip away as I saw how the Divine was providing for me, even with me 'doing' less.

During this time of "cocooning" and learning to 'be', I discovered something else about myself. I learned I am an HSP, a highly sensitive person. This helped me make sense of so many things in my life. Instead of shaming myself for being sensitive and trying to cover it up like I had always done, I began to embrace who I truly was. The sensitive soul in me loves quiet time and time in nature. She is also the one who is creative, intuitive, and spiritual. I began listening and honoring myself and what felt good to me, moment to moment each day.

Listening to my heart led me to let go of everything, and what I found inside was my own fullness, inside me. I learned that I didn't need anything outside myself to feel fulfilled and at peace. Sure, those outside things add pleasure, but it's aligning with my true self, the true me, that brings fulfillment. It feels so good. No more striving, trying to get somewhere, get something, be someone. No more hurrying, busying, producing, performing, or being perfect. I am as I am and it's enough. It's more than enough. What I had been looking for my whole life was fulfillment, and now I had found it, inside of me.

And all those leaps of faith I took in my life, they were all worth it. Especially the most recent one of leaving my career, and going within to find fulfillment. I feel more peace and contentment than I've felt my whole life. It's wonderful to wake up each day, tune into my heart, and listen to what I get to do that day. It's an easy, peaceful and rich way of living. I am so grateful.

~ *Divinity Speaking* ~
"Listening to your heart is the key to fulfillment."

ABOUT THE AUTHOR

JULIE AIRD

Julie Aird is an inspirational speaker, an ICF-credentialed coach, a spiritual director, and the Founder of Julie Aird Life Coaching. She is also the host of the Heart-Led Living podcast.

Driven by her own journey of finding fulfillment within, Julie works with highly sensitive women who have pursued happiness in their career, relationships and family, but are not feeling satisfied. Through powerful energetic and heart-led practices, inner child work, and mindset coaching, Julie's clients experience a profound awakening to an abiding sense of peace and fulfillment within.

Julie lives in Mission Viejo, California, with her husband, Steve, and her son, Jacob.

Website: www.julieaird.com
Facebook: www.facebook.com/groups/fulfillment4sensitivesouls
Instagram: @julie.c.aird
Email: julie@julieaird.com

17

GIVE UP THE LEASH

LINSEY MOSES SMITH

A Change of Plans

*W*hen I first planned to write this chapter, I thought I would share about being married to a psychic and widowed at age thirty-two. Or how as a young girl I used seagulls as divination tools as they flew above the school playground. I thought an upbeat, instructional narrative on how to tune into the divine messages we all have access to would be perfect. And I was so excited to bring those messages to the world! But then...

I got a *dog*.

After being an indoor cat owner for the last sixteen years, it's still a shock to my system to say that. My husband and I had planned to get a dog, but not for another six months or so, after the backyard was finished. After this book launched and I had poured more time into my business. After my elderly cats had stabilized with their health issues and we had given the one on hospice care all the time and love he needed. When my husband, the dog-lover, was ready and found the puppy he wanted *then* we would get a dog. That was the plan. As the saying goes, the best way to make God laugh is to make a plan.

We were three hours away from home for the annual Easter family gathering. It was a large reunion-type weekend with many cousins, aunts and uncles. The second day there, my husband and I joined some cousins on a short road trip to the nearby river for a brief hike. Afterward, we piled back into my cousin's Ford Ranger to head back. Soon I spotted something odd on the other side of the road. An SUV was parked on the shoulder, a woman in the driver's seat on her phone. A large black and brown dog stood outside the car, his paws on her window. The dog seemed frantic and the woman looked stressed. The situation didn't seem right.

I spoke up, calling out the odd scene to my family in the truck. We pulled over and offered to help the lady. "I saw him on the side of the road," she called to us from inside her car. "I'm trying to call animal control." My cousin and husband got out of the car and coaxed the dog over. The dog approached tentatively and peered inside the back seat at me. He met my gaze with sweet blue eyes which seemed to beg for comfort. Within minutes, we were all piled in, and I found myself accepting sloppy kisses from the sixty pound pooch who had made himself comfortable on my lap as we drove toward the local adoption shelter.

Suddenly I heard the thought, *"This is my dog."*

DIVINITY SPEAKS

It was like someone dropped the thought inside my head. The words were phrased as if they came from me, and even though I heard them internally, they felt foreign, not from my mind. I recognized the feeling as I've received these messages before from deceased loved ones, Masters and my Spiritual Support Team. Perhaps clairaudience, perhaps a channeled message, it felt different from regular thoughts which feel like a part of me. This particular thought appeared just above me, in the upper left area by my head. It seemed to not be a part of me, but there it was.

Something about this dog tugged at my heart and now I was hearing that he was MY dog. I had never had this kind of connection with a dog before! The affection I felt for him was instant and surprising. But while the story of Ranger joining our family starts sweetly, *this* message – of Divinity Speaking – is about turbulent times. This is the story of how I up-leveled my intuition. About surrender and alignment.

I obsessed about the dog for the next two weeks. I pushed my husband to discuss adoption and made follow up calls to the shelter. My mind wanted to bring him home but it didn't feel right in my body. I focused only on the eerie, mystical message that "this was my dog" and let fear for his wellbeing drive my thought process. The bad timing was clear from the get-go. I ignored all those signals and things only got worse. My father-in-law going to the ICU two days before our six hour round-trip back to the shelter piled on extra layers of stress and exhaustion that we did not give ourselves time to recover from. We neglected to slow down, discuss and prepare for the changes that were to come, and brought home the dog anyway. The adorableness of our new family member was largely offset by the fact that we knew nothing about him and felt cautious about extending trust too quickly. I was naive about the amount of time, training and attention I had believed it would take to integrate him into our family and was rudely awakened to this fact only by my husband's paranoia that the dog would eat, dig or chew his way to his own demise.

Day one was a fun road trip with our furry new friend, but by day three of having Ranger home, things looked to be falling irreparably apart. What we had thought was an affectionate and gentle, well-behaved pooch was turning out to be a hyper dog with separation anxiety. He didn't know his own strength. The whole arrangement hinged on whether or not he'd be aggressive to our kitties, and Ranger looked hungry. The new schedule of splitting attention between species was overwhelming and relentless. Our mild mannered, elderly cats expressed their rage at the canine invader by hissing at him through the windows and intentionally peeing on both my husband and I. Stressed at being left briefly alone, Ranger destroyed his crate which he had slept in peacefully prior. Frustration peaked as my husband begrudgingly agreed to sleep with him on the cold garage floor that night. As I laid in bed, an anxiety attack set in. Sobbing with regret and guilt, I saw my mistake.

Divinity had spoken to me, literally, and I had trusted it. Yet I had neglected to integrate the message fully before acting. Like a hot tip from the ethers, I had assumed that I must walk this path or miss my chance, ignoring that nothing about it felt right. There, on that third night, with a confused, anxious dog and defeated husband in the garage, two terrified, angry cats next to me, and tears streaming down my cheeks, I realized there was no easy way to fix the situation. The only way out of the mess would be through it.

IN THE FIRE

Though an emotional breakdown over a new pet that came in at a bad time was definitely not the worst I had endured, the stress hormones affected my body the same, and I had to remind myself I'd survived harder things. I forced myself to put those lessons to use. My cheeks still wet with tears, I surrendered the situation to God and prayed not for what I wanted, but for the highest outcome for all involved.

I realized there may have been options that I hadn't explored for the pooch. Perhaps I could have looked further into foster care, or just waited until we were ready and bringing Ranger home felt like a Full

Body Yes, instead of a full-bodied "What the Bleep Did We Do?" Keeping him would be a hard transition for everyone involved; finding him a new home would be a whole other chore with its own heartbreak.

I recognized that I was in the emotional place I call "in the fire" - in the thick of it, a situation full of stress and overwhelm without a visible resolution that felt good. When gold is put in the fire, it is the extreme heat that removes the impurities from the precious metal and purifies it. I remembered that this crisis would yield gold in my life at some point in the future. I cried out my sorrow for imposing so on my family. Surrendering further, I offered up a prayer of gratitude for the shitty situation I had put us all in: gratitude for the person I would become & the growth I would gain through the experience, and for the unknown fruits I trusted would spring from this fertilizer. I desperately busted out a few minutes of breath of fire from my kundalini yoga repertoire to release some of the heavy energy, and eventually fell asleep.

UPLEVEL

This was my advanced lesson on intuition. I had heard spiritual mentors speak of following intuitive hits blindly, to a fault. Of learning to receive messages from Spirit and not acting upon them until they are integrated into the body. Yet I had never experienced it in this way before myself. Usually, my lesson was about having a knowing within me and *not* following it. Those moments of regret for taking someone else's advice instead of listening to my own inner guidance was how I built trust in my intuition and myself. But this was the opposite.

After doing this work for over a decade, I know that aligned guidance from Source comes with ease, flow and inspired action. When we are on the right path, our bodies feel physically relaxed, lit up or expansive - that full body *yes!* Things line up for us and the right timing, people and events fall into place. Worry, doubt and efforting are signals to reevaluate, change direction or wait before proceeding. I knew all of that and yet I still ignored the signs, landing my family smack dab in the middle of chaos, exhaustion and heartache. Though well-intentioned, I trusted a message more than I trusted myself.

WAITING FOR RAINBOWS

I am a firm believer and living example that the biggest challenges in our lives can be the catalyst for beautiful change if we embrace the opportunity presented to us. I have been through many dark times in the past. From struggling through depression to the death of my first husband, and other intense crises that felt like they would never end, I have been surprised by my own strength and willpower. In fact, the greatest versions of myself have come from the growth caused by surviving the worst. Each time when I surrendered to a greater plan, I made space for God to show up. This Divine Intervention *did not change what was*, but rather *changed my perspective* of the event. Like the rainbow after the storm, good things eventually followed.

Often, it takes a while to see what those good things are. We have to trust that they are coming. This process of trust both allows them to show up and gives us hope for a better future while we are still in survival mode. If you were to ask me today what good things came out of Ranger's rough introduction to our family I'm not sure I'd have the right answer yet. The story isn't done. Less than two weeks after he came home, we said goodbye to our sixteen year old Smokey cat who was too frail to weather the changes. It was a heartbreaking blow. And while I know there is a silver lining to all the heartache, (in addition to the love and bond of a new pet) I can't see it yet, and that's ok. I know to trust that the rainbow is coming and that's enough for now.

Hindsight brings a clarity that only comes with time and healing. Understanding that is another type of surrender to the bigger picture. In the meantime, we are enjoying our time with Ranger, our sweet kitty Pele, and the journey of integrating a dog into our family, roller coaster that it is.

GIVE UP THE LEASH

In my crash course on dog behavior, I quickly learned that dogs need a leader. They will sometimes jump up on people, or pull while walking on a leash, or even show aggression all because they think there is no leader. Who the leader is is unclear to them, so they feel forced into being the leader themselves, being in the decision maker role. They manage their situation with unwanted behavior which then causes stress for themselves, not to mention their owners, and surrounding animals or people.

A relaxed, happy dog, however, is a follower. He is a dog that doesn't have to make all the decisions. He knows the pack leader does that. He trusts his leader to guide him. He learns signals and cues and integrates them into his world accordingly. He learns to walk in step, to wait when necessary, and knows to check in with his guide along the way.

It is the same with us and Spirit. Through the hardest times, our stress is multiplied when we believe that we are in the driver's seat, trying to control a situation bigger than ourselves. Though we may not growl at the mailman, we act out our fear, anger and insecurity in other ways when we feel out of control. We feel bad and those around us are affected.

Conversely, when we trust the Universe to lead us we can relax in the knowledge that things are being taken care of, that we are being set up for success. Like handing the leash to God, we get to relax knowing the big stuff is handled, and that even the most stressful situations will come together for our good in the end if we are open to a bigger outcome. The Universe's cues and signals speak to every individual uniquely, but each of us comes with a guidance system pre-installed in the form of our bodies & emotions. We can use this guidance system to discern what direction the leader (Spirit) is prompting us to go. We might receive messages, signs and synchronicities. We may use tools, like oracle cards, pendulums, or angel numbers. But always, ultimate confirmation of any external sign rests *within us*. When we are aligned with our soul's highest direction for us, our emotions feel good, our bodies are lighter. It feels like a breath of fresh air or an exhale. Even a little bit of relief is a big step in the right direction our soul is calling us in.

THE RIPPLE EFFECT

Ok - so what? Why does any of this matter? With the exception of a beloved senior cat, no one died or was rushed to the emergency room. No one went to jail or was struck down by a world-rocking natural or political disaster. And there are plenty of those things happening lately!

Why it matters is exactly that. Our world is shifting, changing. The frequency of crisis in our personal and communal lives seems to be increasing. Perhaps it is just social media that makes it seem so; our awareness of current events happening is more immediate and far-reaching. I prefer to believe that times are *a-changin*! As the energy on the planet rises, that which can not stand the light is revealed to be healed. This creates upheavals in our relationships, communities and governments. So how can we sustain a life of sanity or even joy in this new normal? If the chaos of an eager, well-intended mistake such as mine can wreck so much havoc, how can we make it through the really hard stuff? With practice.

These snafus in life – the ones that maybe aren't really that bad but feel like we're dying while we're in them - are the perfect opportunity. As we practice our alignment, we will be faced with opportunities for healing, growth and expansion.

We get better at alignment by embracing our mistakes. Leaning our awareness gently into the chaos. Loving the hardest moments and getting comfortable being in the fire. By observing the harder emotions that come up with self-awareness and non-judgement, then releasing and moving that lower energy through us. We get better at alignment with acceptance of ourselves, imperfectly perfect. Acceptance of what is, and a kind of, "This is what I'm doing now" mentality. This acceptance is a key step toward the growth and healing we seek.

Our healing is a doorway through which we become new. New versions of ourselves, new parents for our children, new leaders for our communities showing the way to generational change. We lead by example, healing our sh*t and dropping our baggage and mistaken beliefs one by one, or sometimes bucket loads at a time! We practice on the small-but-intensely difficult moments – like rescuing a dog – so we can survive the major, earth shattering ones. And when the dust settles we look around, pat ourselves on the back, and extend a hand to help a friend who is going through their own earth shattering moment. You've survived. And because you did, you know she can too. This is the ripple effect.

JOURNEY HOME

My story of Divinity Speaks and what I thought my message would be has been quite the journey - much like a rowdy dog with sweet blue eyes who went on his own journey and now has a home with us. And much like my own life through this process, which I am honored to share here. We may never know Ranger's origin story but we get to write the rest together.

Life is full of twists and turns, surprises and turbulence. We do our best to align ourselves when Spirit speaks, lean into the fire when things get tough and surrender to a bigger plan. For one dog, and for the whole pack.

~ *Divinity Speaking* ~
"Giving God the leash will lead us home. "

ABOUT THE AUTHOR
LINSEY MOSES SMITH

Linsey Moses Smith is an intuitive author, artist, and Law of Attraction coach. She began working with Energy and Angels in 2009 and has studied Law of Attraction in depth since 2011. Her world opened up when she experienced a series of metaphysical experiences that her religious upbringing could not explain. Linsey helps spiritual seekers who are ready to see their challenges in a new way to shift their perspectives. She is passionate about personal development, emotional intelligence, channeling and Human Design.

Linsey also loves teaching mindfulness and peace education to children, aged pre-school to pre-teens. A former teacher at a triple-accredited school in the San Francisco Bay Area, she blends her Montessori training with spiritual concepts to help children & parents tune into their own intuition for joy and guidance.

She lives in Northern California with her beloved husband, cat Pele and dog Ranger.

Instagram: @linseymosessmith

Facebook: Linsey Moses Smith

Email: linsey.moses.smith@outlook.com

18

YOUR 3PM WEDNESDAY MASSAGE APPOINTMENT

MARDALENA DAWN TURPEL

"*H*ello, I'm Mardalena Dawn, I'll be your massage therapist today. Follow me," I say as I guide you down a dimly lit hallway with lemongrass essential oil floating through the air and the music of White Sun drifting into your ears.

"We'll be in here." I gesture to the door of my healing space. You enter the room, it is peacefully purple and grey, lit with the soft pink glow of a large salt lamp. There is a bench along the wall, a shelf with crystals and a buddha statue and in the center is the massage table.

I follow you in and ask, "Is there anything you would like me to concentrate on or be aware of?"

This is your opportunity to let me know of any pain you feel, any old or recent injuries you have, or where you feel you carry your tension. I ask about how you spend your day, how you move, or don't move, your body for work and for play. After you share with me I will leave you for a few moments while you undress and slide under the soft sheets.

"We'll have you start face down," I motion to the headrest on the top of the table. "I'll give you a few moments, I'll be right back."

"Are you getting comfortable?" I ask as I reenter the space. "Feel free to let me know at any time, if I go too hard or if you would like me to add any additional pressure. Let's begin by taking a deep breath."

Together we draw a long, slow, deep breath in and then slowly release the breath out. I close my eyes and roll them up to my third eye point. I visualize my body emptying, releasing all ego, all intentions, all expectations you or I might have about the outcome of this massage. I visualize becoming an empty vessel.

Then I visualize a golden light pouring through my crown chakra and I pray, "May this healing be for (and then I say your name), may this healing be for your highest good."

Because, even though I have given massages to over 9000 bodies in my twenty-three years of practice, I am wise enough to know that I can't possibly know what is best for you. So I surrender and let divinity speak through my hands.

I continue to model deep breathing to guide the both of us as I compress the long muscles along your spine, stretching your hips and rocking your legs down to your feet. This reminds your body that all the moving parts should be working together harmoniously as one. You are your body and your body is you.

Next, we begin to work with your feet. Our beautifully intricate feet that work so hard for us, physically and energetically. Your feet will give me a reading of what is going on with your whole body through reflexology. Your stiff back muscles? We start to loosen those guys up by rotating and flexing your ankles. Massaging the balls of your feet will start to relax your shoulder blades and when I massage your toes you feel an icy rush of spinal fluid flowing down the back of your neck.

It's all connected. I am always saying this. Emotions, energies, bodies, nerves, skin, blood, meridians. All are pieces of the puzzle that delicately connect our 30 trillion or so cells to form this vessel we call a body. And what connects all those puzzle pieces together, is fascia. Fascia is literally the connective tissue that holds together everything in the body. It is an intelligent, living, extracellular matrix within us. Every single muscle fiber, muscle, nerve cell, body part and our whole bodies are wrapped in fascia. Fascia has layers, like an onion. Fascia is constantly forming and it loses plasticity as we age causing knots or binding muscles together, preventing movement or restricting range of motion. When we move and stretch we are breaking up these layers and softening our fascia physically. When we swallow our emotions or experience trauma; emotional, physical, mental or otherwise, it is within our fascia where it lands and gets stored, emotionally. But this incredible matrix also has the power to support our release of that trauma, those stored, unresolved emotions, that stuck energy or any other congestion that builds up in our bodies. All we have to do is touch it.

Don't believe massage can release backlogged emotions? You don't have to, it's science.

When we are in tune with and leverage this inherent wisdom and infinitely intricate web of intelligence within us, we can gently unwind deeply held patterns, physically and energetically. Want to let 'it' go? That's not a mindset thing, that's a fascia thing.

Before moving on from your feet, I perform a Reiki balancing. Reiki is the practice of channeling energy from the divine and sending it to travel through the energy meridians of your body. My hands warmly cup your ankles and we breathe together. I may see your calves shake or your thighs jump. Sometimes I see a wiggle at the base of your spine, sometimes I don't, but I know the circuit is complete when I see your fingers twitch. Holding space and being witness to this ancient art of channeling energy never fails to move me. It is beautiful, tangible proof of the divine within me and how I can surrender to it to let healing pour through me. I move my hands to cup the balls of your feet and your toes. You reflexively take in a sharp breath. According to reflexology, I am holding your lung area and again, the power of practicing and receiving this ancient wisdom washes over us. I clap my hands to clear the energy and let your body know we are moving on.

Now we move to your back. I use hot towels to warm your skin and gently get your back used to my touch. Working with the fascia lines, or muscles connected by lines of fascia, I begin to create space and movement down your spine, lower back and buttocks. Breaking down the layers of fascia, my hands slide down either side of your spine, down your butt and around the front of your hips. We take a long deep breath together as my hands glide back up the sides of your body.

You can feel the layers of fascia ripple and soften beneath my fingers as I slowly sweep under your armpits then compress flat hands toward and up your neck, resting at the base of your skull. We repeat this three times together. This helps to free the connections around the scapula, which is a bone not connected to other bones but held to the body completely by soft tissue. It also helps to loosen the fascia cages around your shoulders, chest and hips which bind those areas together and can prevent the release of lower back tension and cause the slumping shoulders effect.

My hands work simultaneously together and separately, playing your body like a piano. One hand manipulates the tissue while the other operates as a stabilizer or distractor. Both hands deftly switching roles as the divinity within you guides the divinity flowing through them.

"You know just how to find all my spots," you say.

"It's not me," I reply. "It's your spirit dancing with mine. You are leading me with your own divine knowing about how to heal your body. I simply get the privilege of listening."

For your arms and shoulders, I dangle your arm over the side of my massage table and kneel on the floor beside you. With a generous amount of coconut oil, I let the power of gravity help ease the tension in your shoulders and neck as I cradle your elbow in my left arm. My right hand slips under your armpit around your collar bone and holds the tension along the top of your shoulder with pressure absent of force until the tension begins to melt away beneath my fingers. Pressure without force is key to releasing the painful tension. You have to meet the pain to release the pain, I quietly tell you. We breathe deeply together.

After both sides are complete, I clap my hands to clear the energy and let your body know we are moving on. We complete your back treatment with a Reiki balancing where I place one hand on the small of your back and the other on the base of your head and neck and again I pray to let this healing be for your highest good. Then I ask you to flip over. You didn't think I was going to forget your head and neck, did you?

I leave the juicy releases of the neck to the end for many reasons. By this time in the massage our energies have had a chance to dance and play together and your body has developed some trust of my touch. This will allow us to work deeper to achieve more release together. Deeper release means more relief from your pain.

Let's take a look at what is happening to our bodies in the hunched over, computer desk posture many of us carry. Our hard working neck and shoulder muscles in the back get overextended while our front neck and shoulder muscles get hyper constricted. Both are super tight but in opposite ways. Our neck muscles are trying to help us balance our heads 24/7, even while we are sleeping! Aside from being terribly physically painful, this is an energetic tragedy because it restricts or closes off our heart and throat chakras. So many of us are walking around disconnected from our heart center and robbed of the power of our true voices.

I spend some gentle but firm moments breaking up the fascia web around the front of your throat down into your rib cage. It is an awkward feeling for you and painful, maybe even a little scary. You are not used to your throat being touched and you were not aware of the tension you chronically kept there. In a moment of fear you debate asking me to stop but the fear passes with the melting of the pain. After the physical manipulations, we take another long, slow, deep breath.

I perform a Reiki balancing over your ears, head and shoulders. I feel the warm energy traveling from one hand, through your body, and back to my other hand. We experience this circuit of energy in a moment free from time.

I employ the deep, cooling, pain relieving powers of blue chamomile, peppermint and spearmint essential oils so you can carry the healing of this experience with you after you leave our space and throughout the rest of your day.

To end our time together, I pick up my tuning fork tuned to 528 Hz, the frequency of love. I chime the fork and place it over your heart chakra.

"This is 528 Hz," I say. "This is the vibrational frequency of love. Love for your body." I move the fork over your throat chakra. "Love for yourself." I chime the fork again and move it over your third eye chakra. "Love for your experience." I chime it one last time and swirl it over your crown chakra.

"Thank you very much," I say.

You can't bypass this human experience to have a spiritual one. Being human *is* the spiritual experience. With grace and forgiveness, I ask you to embrace the times you peed in your pants accidentally or resorted to using manipulation to get what you wanted, the times you lost patience with yourself or your loved ones or you flaked on an appointment you wanted to attend or when you failed to commit to that change you were trying to make. These aspects are just as much a part of you as the bright and shiny parts and deserve your love, compassion and acknowledgement. Once you shine a light for yourself on these not so flashy facets and become intimately acquainted with them as YOU (YOU are THEM and THEY are YOU), it's not so scary anymore for others to see these parts of you. The fear of being identified solely as someone who pees their pants begins to dissipate because you know that while you might have lost control of your bladder that one time (or every other time you laugh) that is only one small part of the beautifully complex dance your soul energy will display here on Earth.

Thank you, again. It was my pleasure to share this space with you. Drink a lot of water and you might feel a little sore in the places we went deeper, like you had a good workout. I'll see you next Wednesday at 3pm.

~ Divinity Speaking ~
"Your pursuit of honesty will scare people and you will be disrespected for it. People will fear your willingness to address your pain, they will dismiss you as weak. You will be brutally critiqued by your oppressors as you discover the keys to your freedom. This is your life, don't miss out on living your most magical experience for them!"

ABOUT THE AUTHOR

MARDALENA DAWN TURPEL

Mardalena Dawn Turpel is the owner-operator of Mardalena's Massage in San Ramon, California. She is a Master intuitive massage therapist, podcast producer and host and award winning international best selling author of *Lineage Speaks* and *Prosperity Codes*. In her 23 years of experience she has massaged over 9,000 bodies and she combines this experience with her vast knowledge of fascia and kinesiology to customize every massage session to tailor to her clients specific needs and goals. She helps her clients living with chronic pain or discomfort, transform their relationships with their bodies from one of pain to one of pleasure. She believes it is never too late to change your story and reconnect to the divinity inside you.

Instagram: @Mardalenadawnsmassage

Facebook: Mardalena's Massage

Email: Mardalenadawn@gmail.com

19

THE GIRL WITH THE COSMIC ROADMAP

MELISSA LAMBOUR

The Girl with the Cosmic Roadmap

"*E**very person deserves a place to call home, whether it's on this earth or within their soul.*" - from my chapter, "Beyond Labels: Finding Your Place in the World" in *Legacy Speaks*

"Maiaaaaa...Have you eaten?" screamed one of her mothers.

Affection was shown through food in her household. Chilis, cilantro and fruit seasoning were their common ground. Her Thai/Malaysian mom sprinkled tamarind chili powder over her fruit, while her Guatemalan/Peruvian mom sprinkled a *pepita* chili lime mix. Just like their personalities, one was sweet and sour, the other salty and sour, but always fiery. They were both foodies, constantly battling it out as to who had the best dish. Every dish was carefully crafted to honor the origin of the recipe and the ingredients.

She wondered how it would be with her birth parents. All she knew was that her biological parents were immigrants, her mother from Egypt and her father from Peru. She ended up in foster care after her parents died in a horrific car accident, leaving her all alone without any family in the US. The only thing foster care saved from her parent's belongings was a scroll that opened up to an elaborate world map with Arabic writing and astrological symbols. She knew that the seven star cluster on the map referred to Pleiades and she was named after one of the stars, Maia, mother of Mercury, Roman god of commerce, communication, and travel. To her surprise, her foster moms owned a Subaru, which also meant Pleiades, but in Japanese.

At least her foster mom could fill her in on her Peruvian side, along with living near Little Lima in Paterson, New Jersey. She struggled to connect with her Egyptian side, even though her neighborhood in South Paterson was predominantly Middle Eastern, Turkish and North African. She spoke both Spanish and Arabic, but neither at a level that gave her confidence in her language skills. She was often misidentified as Dominican and rarely accepted as her true lineage, Egyptian or Peruvian. Maia's parents did an excellent job exposing her to many cultures, but didn't anticipate her feeling even more disconnected.

She felt a deep connection to the earth and the cosmos throughout her life. Even though she felt completely disconnected from her blood lineage, she found comfort in knowing that we all come from stardust. On any given night, you'd find her staring up at the sky, trying to catch a glimpse of a shooting star. She knew this map she inherited had a message for her. Who could help her understand this map and unlock the true powers passed down to her? Would it allow her to go from astral projection to teleportation?

Intuitively she began astral projection by connecting with her chakras and incorporating artifacts from places around the world. She had a vast collection of crystals and textiles to harness the energy of certain places from afar. She would reference her map often, but she knew it wasn't being used to its fullest capabilities.

"Maia!!! Someone's at the door for you!" she heard from downstairs.

Who was it? She never got any visitors. She tried to peek from the top of the stairs, but couldn't get a good look at the unexpected visitor.

She threw on something more presentable than her constellation pajamas, and made her way down the stairs with the ease of a lioness.

"Heyyy, Soraya!" Maia greeted her visitor nervously. She finally understood what "butterflies in your stomach" meant. From the first day that Soraya appeared as the new girl at her school, she had this weird effect on her. They had barely spoken in class up to that point. So, why was she at her house?!

"Would you like to come up to my room?" Maia was excited to show off her crystal collection and oracle cards.

Soraya lit up at the offer and followed Maia up the stairs.

"I can't believe it! You have my favorite book!" Soraya pointed to *Allah, Liberty and Love: The Courage to Reconcile Faith and Freedom* by Irshad Manji. "This book helped me normalize the feelings I was having."

"What feelings?" Maia asked, but she already knew where this was going.

"The feelings I have towards YOU!" Soraya smiled flirtatiously as she moved closer to Maia.

Maia's mind began racing. Irshad Manji was a beacon of hope for her and so many in the Muslim LGBTQIA+ community. This was the first time her sexuality came into question. She had never been attracted to anyone up to that point. Even though her moms were lesbians, she never considered if she could be Queer.

"Oh wow, I'm so flattered!" Maia blurted out as her body quivered. But as she peered into Soraya's eyes, she instantly felt at ease, and knew this felt like "home."

"What's this scroll?" Soraya stretched out the map and immediately saw the Seven Sisters star cluster. "Did you know my name means "The Seven Sisters" or Pleiades in Persian?! It's *Al-thurayya* in Arabic, but *Soraya* in Persian."

Maia couldn't help but see the Pleiades connection. Were they Pleiadian Starseeds? She was ready to be a star in her galaxy. She was, Maia, one of the Seven Sisters of Soraya. Maia had finally found "home."

As they both touched the scroll, it began to light up like it never had before. That was the moment Maia realized Soraya was the missing puzzle piece!

"Let's see what this map can do!" Maia said as she jumped into action. Pulling out her astral travel journal to take note of the symbols that would light up. She had a feeling this map was meant to bring her closer to the cosmos. This was her "Cosmic Roadmap."

Maia began pointing at places, first her ancestral connections: Egypt and Peru and then her cosmic connection: Japan. She had always been drawn to Japan and its culture, which also made her wonder if she had some Japanese ancestry from her Peruvian side.

"I knew it when I saw all the *Manga* on your walls!" Maia blushed as she glanced over at the Japanese comics. Soraya continued in awe, "My plan is to travel to Japan the first moment I get after High School. I've even studied Japanese these past few years."

"I often astral travel to Japan when I'm stressed." Maia shared how each astral trip allows her to harness the energy of Japan. Her hand was still over Japan on her Cosmic Roadmap. It began to show a blue line and what appeared as the symbol for the Moon. The Moon corresponds to the energy of home and family. Was this her future home, the one that her soul has been yearning for?

Soraya placed her hand over Japan and a yellow line appeared with the symbol for the Sun. The Sun corresponds to the energy of illumination and fame. Is this where she would finally get recognized for her art?

"You know, what this means?! You are my Sun and I am your Moon. You bring the light to awaken my soul and illuminate my path."

Three months had passed since Soraya was the new kid at school. Her relationship with Maia was getting intense. She had done a good job of hiding it from her parents and was so grateful that Maia's parents understood everything they were going through. It was written in the stars for them to meet and expand each other.

Soraya softly kissed Maia goodbye on her lips as they left school, "I guess I'll see you tomorrow?"

Maia responded, "Of course, silly! Why wouldn't I see you?" They hugged and parted ways.

Soraya had a bad feeling as she entered her front door. All she could hear in her head was Maia asking "Why wouldn't I see you?" in an endless loop. Her body prepared for the worst!

"Soraya, can you explain this in your journals?" her father pointing to her most personal entries. She knew this was the end for her. Her strict Iranian parents disapproved of her sexual fluidity. They didn't understand why she couldn't just conform to "normal" beauty standards of a young woman set by society. They saw her short hair as a protest against femininity. Up to that point they had kept their opinions to themselves, but now with her deepest secrets exposed, she couldn't deny her truth.

"*Baba*, I'm so sorry, but I love her!"

Her dad shook his head in disbelief, while her mom cried helplessly. "I have no choice, but to send you to your *ameh*, my sister in LA!"

Soraya felt her heart leap out of her chest. Time stopped and she couldn't hear anything else her father had to say. She was about to leave the only home she ever knew.

She was numb and didn't know how she made it to her bedroom. She stared at her phone, typing nonsense, only to delete it immediately. This went on for hours.

Meanwhile, Maia noticed Soraya's indecisive text. The typing notification would go on and off, on and off. What was Soraya trying to say?

"My love, I don't know how to say this, but my parents found out about us and are sending me to LA. I leave tonight!" Soraya could barely type through her tears. She convinced her mom to bring her to Maia's to say goodbye. It was all her dad's doing to send her off to her aunt's house in *Tehrangeles*, AKA Little Persia, a cultural hub for the Persian community in Los Angeles since the 1960s.

Soraya's dad thought she had become the product of her environment in lower middle-class New Jersey. He thought private school in LA would help her snap out of this "phase." However, the joke was on him since she was about to enter Queer Persian Heaven. The lesbian show, The L-Word, set in LA, paved the way for Queer visibility in the Persian community.

Soraya's aunt answered the door, "*Azizam*, my dear! I can't believe how much you have grown! How was your flight?"

"Fine, I'm just tired." Soraya couldn't help, but stare at the gold detail and exquisite mosaic work throughout the house. This was luxury she never experienced back in Paterson.

"I know why your father sent you to live with me!" Soraya perked up in fear. "But you don't have to worry! You are free to live your truth here!" Soraya eased back into her body once she realized she manifested the perfect place to continue exploring and expressing her sexuality.

"Can I call my girlfriend?" Soraya asked her aunt in great relief.

"Of course, *Azizam*! How beautiful! What is her name?"

"Maia! She completes me, like *Maia* in *Soraya*." They both laughed at the Soraya/Seven Sisters/Pleiades reference.

The weeks that followed, Maia finally managed to teleport from NJ to California by using her activated Cosmic Roadmap. Whether it was Little Tokyo to enjoy their mutual love of Japanese culture or hangout at the beach to watch the pelicans and the seals, Maia couldn't wait for the next adventure with Soraya. Los Angeles gave them the freedom to be themselves and tap into the cultures that brought out the Moon in Maia and the Sun in Soraya.

"Soraya, *habibti*, you are my Sun and I am your Moon. My soul is forever ignited by your light."

"*Yalla*, Maia, let's go off to our next adventure!"

⁊

"Do you ever meet people and wonder why you're so drawn to them? They may carry or embody the planetary energies you were destined to connect with." - from my chapter, "Beyond Lineage: Our Cosmic Connection" in *Lineage Speaks*

I invite you to go back through all my chapters in the She Speaks Series. Each chapter revealed my purpose and helped me shed the years of shame I carried for things I had no control over, like my sexuality. The moment I awakened sexually, my whole life started falling into place. It felt like my spirituality and creativity had no bounds moving forward. In *Legacy Speaks*, I shared my non-linear journey into Astrogeography. In *Lineage Speaks*, I explained my ancestral connection to the cosmos that now allows me to help others understand their own unlikely, cosmic connections to people, places and things around the world. In my own search for belonging, I learned that I had to accept and forgive myself before I expected anyone else to.

Once I faced the world unapologetically, my lived experience no longer had to hide in the depths of my psyche. The weight I carried all those years was finally lifted, allowing me to dive back into my body. I began to understand my chakras with energetic tools like Reiki and Ayurveda, and discovered that my inner flame had long been extinguished by the rain of my sorrows. I stoked that fire again by aligning with all the things that lit up my soul. Travel opened my eyes and heart to different ways of living and connecting. It was inevitable that my business, my legacy, my life's work, would ultimately guide spiritual nomads back to themselves, their purpose, and their place in this world.

This chapter of *Divinity Speaks* was meant to go beyond the scope of my reality, while being set in places that felt familiar. "The Girl with the Cosmic Roadmap" allowed me to weave in my lived and learned experiences across all the characters. It shows that we can all find a piece of ourselves in each other, regardless of the labels. We are forever connected by the cosmos!

Just like Maia in the story, I developed my own Cosmic Roadmap with Astrogeography to understand myself and how I relate to the world. As a child of divorced immigrant parents, I often felt disconnected from my roots and sought family or "home" in the most unlikely places. Astrogeography made me realize that the people I attracted and the cultures I was drawn to, were supposed to bring me a sense of "home" where I didn't feel it in my own family or community. Our families may disown or disapprove of our existence like Soraya experienced in the story. The concept of "chosen" family is nothing new in the Queer community for the sake of safety and living authentically. Every Queer story is a beacon of hope for those that have lost all hope within their own families. I resonated deeply with Queer Muslim stories due to the many parallels to my strict Catholic upbringing. The power of those stories led me on an inward journey to loving myself, releasing shame, and honoring my desires.

My chosen family, my cosmic family was waiting for me with open arms!

My life is a testament that things *will* get better. Even if you've had to leave your family to live your truth, find solace in the fact that your cosmic family is around the world waiting for you. You are never alone, you will always have someone, someplace, or something to lean on. I am now taking the leap of faith to travel my own Cosmic Roadmap. I left my engineering career of over 13 years, so I could fully commit to this life of travel and cosmic connections. I'm choosing to leave the comfort of a career and stable relationship, in order to experience the world through my eyes and heart. Every person I encounter will be a portal into the next phase of my evolution.

There's power of "choice," whether it's family, where to live or a partner. We always have a choice to change our reality or create the life of our dreams. I lead an unconventional life, where I choose to love many and align myself with the frequency of love. That is why I am starting my journey along my Venus line in Spain. Venus energy is all about love, whether it's for yourself, others, or the things you do and surround yourself with. This next phase in life, I'm letting love lead. The more we do things with love, the more aligned we'll be with our purpose and place in the world. You'll notice that the people you attract will require less convincing and less energy than your old friends. In the end, we are all energetic beings, seeking inner and outer balance in our interactions.

I am the Girl with the Cosmic Roadmap! My adventure awaits. New loves, new experiences, new lessons, new stories to write about. By choosing the path least taken, I'm stretching myself in order to heal my lineage. I will travel along my harmonious planetary lines to harness the energy of each place. Each place unlocking more of my purpose and widening my perspective. The richness of my life will be measured by the quality of my connections and experiences. I will continue to interview people through my Cosmic Roadmap Podcast and allow that to evolve into a video blog series as I travel around the world. Eventually my bestselling novels will be flying off the shelves and my stories will turn into blockbusters. My stories will bring life and hope into this world. I've rewritten my trajectory to align with my soul, not the expectations of my family, culture or society.

There's a fire within me that can't be tamed, no matter how much water you throw at me to put out the flames. I've weathered many storms and choose to stoke my own fire along with the fire of others around me. Community is what I seek moving forward. We can't depend only on ourselves. Healing myself has been essential to fill my cup to the brim, so my connections are not meant to complete me, but rather complement and amplify the greatness I already possess.

~ Divinity Speaking ~
"I lean into the fire...
The flames of my desire...
You throw water onto my flame...
But I harness the power of my pain...
Allowing the mist and smoke to rise up high...
And my flames to burn brighter and roar louder into the sky!"

ABOUT THE AUTHOR

MELISSA LAMBOUR

Melissa Lambour is a spiritual globetrotter that turned her wanderlust into her life's work when she became a Reiki AstroGeo Guide and founded Cosmic Roadmap. She guides the endless wanderer to discover their place in the world with her signature Astrogeography sessions. Weaving together Reiki, Ayurveda and Astrogeography, she has helped digital nomads and avid travelers develop a Cosmic Roadmap that determines their next steps in life and business.

She strives to serve people from all walks of life, especially individuals belonging to the 2SLGBTQIA+, BIPOC and immigrant communities that have felt out of place or called to travel the world. She has also traveled to over twenty countries and holds a BE/ME in Mechanical/Biomedical Engineering and an MBA in Sustainability Management with thirteen years of career experience. You'll find her living her best life around the world as she follows her own Cosmic Roadmap.

Tune into her travel podcast, Cosmic Roadmap.

Cosmic Roadmap: www.cosmicroadmap.com

Instagram: @melissalambour

20

SPIRIT IS HERE FOR YOU ALWAYS
IF YOU ARE OPEN

NICOLE HANLON REID

I was ten years old the first time I clearly remember hearing my spirit guides speak to me. I was sat at the desk in my bedroom doing homework when I heard my name being called. I got up from my chair, opened the door, and called out in response down the hall to where my family were. But all I got back in return was confusion, as they said they had not called out for me. A bit confused but certain I had heard my name being called, I sat back down at my desk. Not a moment went by when I heard the call again. This time I was sure someone was playing a trick on me. But once more I was met with confusion and now a little laughter as my family thought I was going a little mad. When the third call came I walked down the hall to look my mother in the eye so she could see I was serious. She came back with me to my room and said, "it may just be the wind blowing through your window," but as she went to close it she realised it wasn't open. A brief moment of wonder passed over her face and I waited to see what other explanation she had for me. But she just turned and said she was sure it was nothing and encouraged me to finish my homework, and so I did.

Fast forward to the next day, where at the end of school I would be met by my father, standing at the school gate waiting on my sister and me. Now, you have to understand this was a man who usually worked such long hours we didn't see him each day until well after 6 pm, so you can understand why the very sight of him told me something was wrong. He smiled and tried to act as normal as possible for this unusual situation, but once in the car, he turned around to tell my sister and I that my Grandma, the maternal matriarch of our family, the "Chief" as she was endearingly referred to, had died. I remember him preparing us for my mother's upset but reassuring us that she would be ok. There were many tears shed and plans made for my mother to return to the UK, where our extended family lived. At some point that night, none of us can remember exactly when, I remembered the voice calling to me, and I knew it had been her. My mother did the UK to Canada time difference and confirmed that yes the timelines did in fact line up. At that moment I felt an overwhelming sense of calm knowing that divine spirits are with us always; reaching out to speak to us and guide us in all that we do.

I spent the next couple of years feeling deep joy and connection going to church and saying my prayers, with this knowledge in my heart. I would see and feel spirit all around me and would go on to share this story with great awe for many years, as the night my grandmother's spirit came to visit me as she passed. However, despite this, it would be tainted only two years later when I would be rocked to my core by the significant death of my Aunt, which would leave me with a huge crisis of faith and consumed in grief. Unfortunately, life would go on to present me with a further three significant deaths within a space of four years, which would lead me to push my spirit team away in anger.

In the few years following this string of deaths, I looked for sources of physical pain to give reason to my internal ones by self-harming. I would burn and scratch my skin just enough to give my logical mind something to show for how I felt inside, without harming myself enough to draw too much attention from others. I drank alcohol and smoked cannabis to numb it and found myself being whoever I thought others wanted me to be, never fully being myself. I was filled with feelings of uncertainty and questioned the Divine's higher power well into my late twenties. My heart, mind, and intuition were at odds with one another. On one hand, I continued to feel connected to a higher power but on the other, trusting in it, amongst all the grief, left me feeling let down and hurt by God. As if he were to blame for taking these loved ones from me without consideration of the emotional impact and that it was spirit who could make this pain go away, but didn't. This inner battle would lead me to slowly distance myself from church and hide my spirituality as I felt ashamed and embarrassed of it. I would begin to question God's hand in more and more disasters in the world, wondering how he could allow these things to continue to happen.

I also developed anxiety, which was often triggered by making unsafe choices. This anxiety grew and became panic attacks, which left me on many occasions in my early twenties and into my thirties, unable to breathe, in a blur, on the floor in everyday situations and unsure what the trigger had been. During this time I didn't open myself to spirit, I rejected any nudges I may have felt and I didn't look to hear their guidance. Instead, I forged through life working hard to reach my goals in the logical practical way I thought everyone pushed through.

In my late twenties, I moved back to Scotland and although I still brought a lot of my poor decision-making with me initially, I began to feel myself soften and feel the call from spirit a little stronger. The true me slowly began to find space and along with it, I was gifted almost daily with white feathers, as a reminder that I was not alone. I also began to see butterflies all the time, which was my Aunt's favourite animal and I knew these visits were her way of sharing messages with me. I also began to hear spirit through song and lyrics once more, somehow always hearing the right message whenever I needed it to guide me to my next right steps.

Then, my desire to find a place within a faith community where I felt welcome came calling. At my very first service back, it was as if the sermon that day was written just for me. Every line the priest spoke was like being welcomed home, and the service ended with my very favourite hymn, 'Here I am Lord' which brought tears to my eyes. These events and some important conversations about my losses would swing the door to spirit wide open and I would feel fully connected once again.

I now live my life with the peace of knowing I am never alone and the trust that I am led by something greater than myself. It's allowed me to accept all of me and know that if the divine spirit loves and believes in me, then I can too.

Leaning into my Intuition and feelings of deep knowing is now core to how I live my life and run my business. By offering up prayers of gratitude and openness to spirit, and using angel cards and tarot cards each day, I welcome any guidance they have for me and I am never let down. Working with intuition in this way is one of the pillars of the authentic living techniques that I lead people through and I find it to be so powerful. For me trusting in the whispers and nudges, takes me from uncertainty, nervousness, and anxious feelings - to calm confidence, peace, happiness, and inner knowing. No matter how the whisper comes, once I receive a message from the divine, my soul feels reassured and I can clearly and confidently take my next steps, trusting that there is always a plan. I believe that every unanswered prayer is a gift from the divine because they can see the bigger picture and that something greater is coming your way.

Even as I sat and wrote this chapter I asked my spirit team to guide me to write the words that needed to flow through me and that needed to be heard. When I did I was intuitively led to use certain essential oils, which I would later look up and learn are for supporting higher connection. I also pulled the Akasha card, with the message; your guidance is divinely guided. This is the type of interaction I have with spirit daily and I feel so grateful for it. I will never be closing that door again because with it open I am more myself and more whole than ever.

~ Divinity Speaking ~
"Trust in your intuition, as all you seek is already within you."

ABOUT THE AUTHOR

NICOLE HANLON REID

Nicole Hanlon Reid aka Nicole H.R is a Mindfulness Master Practitioner, Emotional Well-being coach, and essential oil educator. She blends these modalities and her authentic living technique to empower busy working women to calm their nervous systems and tap into the present moment to activate emotional healing through the everyday chaos. Her clients release negative emotional patterns such as self-judgment and experience lasting shifts.

Nicole's mission is to help more women embody authenticity, self-acceptance, and self-confidence, to create a lifestyle unique to their true desires.

Nicole is a Scottish-born, Canadian-bred, busy Mum of two, currently living in Scotland. She loves traveling, and connecting in nature with her family, and is passionate about doing what she can to combat climate change.

Instagram: @nicole_h.r

Facebook: www.facebook.com/hanlon1

LinkedIn: www.linkedin.com/in/nicole-h-r-35b36a245

21

A DELICACY OF AWARENESS

SUZANNE NICHOLE PRESTON

Presence
Awareness
Trust
Intuition
Surrender
Flow
Every move, every word, every action

PRESENCE

*K*eep *Observing, until you enter the soul's domain. Here you witness the presence of spirit in everything you see, hear, smell, taste and touch.*

Present, the moment felt like my first immersion in water, though more refined than crawling into the sea to eat sand. My daily swim, breath, body, mind & spirit entwined in a beautiful dance, effortlessly, freely, gliding through and with water, was a reset. An enjoyable routine I like to name Mermaid Duties. I must admit I was a little obsessive at one point but sometimes we've got to go there... you know, to extremes, to gain experiential knowledge of whatever it is. I'll elaborate on how my daily interaction with water got disrupted a little later. A moment that led me to realise that routines (if one was to be judgmental, even perceived good ones) we place in our lives can limit us from any other possibility or opportunity. In a way we create resistance to the *flow*. Water is one of my great teachers; observing it, being immersed in it, gliding through it and floating on it. One can only surrender to such an incredible force of nature, we can't resist it, that would be futile and a massive waste of energy.

Mid mermaid duties, sensing I was nearing the edge of the water's container, goggles steamed, I paused to clear them. A muffled sound vibrated through my silicone ear plugs, the voice came from the adjacent lane, "you look like you're doing ballet when you swim, it's mesmerising". I pondered for a moment. I have been told this many times, grateful for the comment and so happy that others have an awareness of the simple things. (I rarely witness this alertness in the city.) I replied "Thank you. Graceful?" a cheeky glint in my eye,

"No, better. It's like watching a ballet...".

I laughed, reflecting on what process or internal action gives it that aesthetic or external property. When one is truly *present*, immersed in the *moment* there is an ease, a fluidity, *flow* an effortless beauty. Often, I see this in the way birds navigate the air and in dancers as the body moves momentarily through space and time. Swimming feels this way,

"Swimming to me is a meditation. I'm present throughout the process, with *a delicacy of awareness*. Fascinated by every subtle micro movement, the sound of my breath an epic theme tune. I observe the water's playful, geometric patterns rippling away from me and back towards me, it drops me into a deeply connected state". Those words flowed out of me, the Merman (I'm assuming he labels himself as such) humoured me with a smile "It's just nice to watch".

AWARENESS

Awareness is a process of full concentration. A process of clear analytic action on the points you deal with in a particular moment. This fascinates me.

Post mermaid duties, I chose to stroll the alluring, beautiful route to the apartment. Apparently, it takes longer. Present, the experience called me. Longer, shorter, in the moment I'll get to the same space at the right time. Considering Manchester was the hub of the last Industrial Revolution and is rapidly becoming the next smart city, somehow, miraculously I find pockets of nature hidden amongst old warehouses, the city/building site and the rapidly growing skyward landscape. There is so much beauty in the river route; a symphony of melodic bird song, lush leafy green upon green, greens I've never seen. Ethereal dandelion puff balls shed fairy fluff, lightness fills the air, reminding me of the magic that is. In contrast the city has a grey tinge, a density. The hypnotising sound, constant action and darkness can distract. Subconsciously it draws you in, hence choosing the airy, scenic route that afternoon.

TRUST

Belief is theoretical. Trust is existential

— OSHO, LIVING DANGEROUSLY

Was it the route or my perspective?

With a different perspective I could've chosen to place foot in front of foot, entirely unaware of nature's beauty, adaptability and resilience. It amazes me how plants advance from perceived solid brick walls under sombre railway arches.

Nature's Divine enchanting forms blow me away, no resistance to the universal intelligence, with an absolute *trust*, it allows. Why do we so often get in the way then? Is it through societal conditioning? A lack of *trust*? A belief so concrete that something outside of ourselves is in charge? A fear that leads to grasping onto the little control we believe we have. It makes sense, since throughout his story we have been manipulated to look or worship something outside of us, distracted, disconnected and conditioned to feel disempowered.

I wonder if the absence of *presence*, *awareness* and *trust* alongside the disconnection from our external and internal environment, leads to the blame mentality we see ingrained in the world today. The old system and way of living, with its structure, limitations, separation and fear-based control has taken us further away from *trusting* our own power and the universal Divine energy. What changes when we reconnect the mind, body & spirit, take ownership, trust our intuition and *trust* we are one with the universe? That we are co-creators, we are Divinity?

What happens when we shift from, I AM my name, I AM the labels, I Am the limiting beliefs, both personal and those put upon us to I AM present now, connected to the infinite energetic field, powerful beyond imagination?

We are Divine bioelectromagnetic beings. Our brain & central nervous system is electrical. Our body is 70% conscious salt water, allowing electricity to flow. We have seven chakras to generate electricity & seven glands to convert it to energy for the body. We have energy meridians to move energy within the body. The breath, pretty crucial, brings in oxygen which fuels & flows the energy. There is an infinite amount of Energy available to us and the body, a beautiful container for our spiritual experience, holds this energy - our energy - together and creates a living space for the soul.

In ordinary awareness, we see the obvious. But with *a delicacy of awareness*, we go beyond the apparent, piercing the mask of appearances, into the field of light where spirit shines, and everything connects. We sense our connection with this energy. No longer bound by five senses, divinely guided, in an effortless *flow*, no resistance, no desire to control. In this fluid state is a great amount of freedom and the magic starts to unfold.

INTUITION

To truly trust our intuition, we must first trust ourselves.

My original intention was to tell you the simple story of how my connection, life practice and ever evolving relationship with the physical body has given me deep experiential knowledge, unbound by logic of the Divine (call it what you want, but for the purposes of this it has that label). Learning how to point and flex my feet in baby Ballet classes was one element of my journey. An exploration of dance, dedication to my yoga practice and immersing myself in other disciplines; Chi Kung, Pilates, Martial Arts, Somatic work, Feldenkrais, Reiki, Meditation, consciousness exploration in floatation tanks, gong meditations, trusting gravity in aerial arts, the list goes on. I found by trusting my physical body, organically I became aware of the formless body - the limitless, the unfathomable - then I started trusting my *intuition*. But I wondered if I could apply the knowledge learnt through movement, flow and entering a space with no resistance, to the way I live? On this adventure, I also noted that in many cultures, traditions and teachings, we're working the same systems, but with a different approach. Regardless of approach, what happens when we consciously integrate these practices into daily life?

I often forget how much discipline and effort has gone into clearing; letting go physically, mentally and emotionally, combined with strengthening my system in order to allow the powerful force that *is* to flow effortlessly through me. It's felt too much on many occasions, but I've continued. My soul is shining through with such beauty, who am I to limit it, we're on this journey together, I now trust it. For years I resisted this, the fear of how powerful I could be genuinely frightened me. That, and a fear of not having control. Can we ever have control though? Could control simply be seen as a choice? Letting go of learnt behavioural patterns, surrender, trust and a refining of my awareness has allowed my *intuition* and *multisensory* system to become my life's GPS.

Though I'd love for every interaction to be beautiful (it is in some manner), I admit, I've kicked doors down with a less than graceful air. Acting from a fear-based state rather than one of trust. When chaotic elements of urban life seep in; the external pressure to be, achieve and attain something in the future, both inner and outer contradiction after contradiction surface from murky depths. Waves of overwhelm crash over me, a waterfall of emotions cascade and My GPS gets glitches. It hurts hard to witness both the magnificent beauty and unsighted destruction simultaneously. The simplicity of being versus the human condition. That alongside the simple call to pay the rent, enjoy life and live with some integrity. Navigating life can become messy when we're nudged away from our *intuition*, regardless of glitches and though often it feels against tide, the path of ease is aligned with the Divine.

SURRENDER

It is enough that one surrenders oneself. Surrender is to give oneself up to the original cause of one's being. Do not delude

yourself by imagining such source to be some God outside you.
One's source is within oneself. Give yourself up to it.

— SRI RAMANA MAHARSHI *(A TREASURY*
OF TRADITIONAL WISDOM)

What happens when we surrender? Intuitively I'm veering away from my original intention, which I would love to elaborate on, but I feel moments in daily existence often bring us deeper knowledge.

In one explosive moment, I was reminded of the importance of *surrender* an element I feel is needed in order (or disorder) for us to live with and in alignment with *nature*. A moment that impacted my routine, disrupted my daily swim and was most likely the catalyst to writing this.

Forget me not, it was a Slovenian sparkling wine that got my attention. Yes, I am fully aware many yogis appear to live off kale juice and air. I absolutely love kale and air but remain authentic, happy to enjoy this 3D experience choosing not to buy into Spiritual correctness or the wellness industry monopolising individual's insecurities.

Forget me not, yes it made me look twice. Drew me in. Its name! And I haven't! Though I never tasted it, it made a lasting impact. In a thirty-minute mid-morning gap between teaching clients and attending a session I flip flopped out of the apartment, taking the mini river route, purse and phone in hand, to the newly opened supermarket down the road. Shades on to dim the super bright isles and the hypnotising-coloured packaging filled with predominantly processed junk, gliding through the Isle, I picked up the kale I went in for;) But so intrigued by this bottle enroute to the check-out, I placed it in my basket. Pressurised containers on occasion explode.

FLOW

Make it conscious

I'd delicately placed *Forget me not* on the check-out counter, still enchanted by its name and transfixed by the bottles contour, I pivoted to pick up other items in the basket behind me.

An explosion. Glass fragments shimmered across the space with matrix style effects, sunlight penetrating through the window enhancing the cinematic ambience, shrapnel liberated across the floor. No sensation (pain would be the first that springs to mind, based on conditioning... and a lazy nervous system). A knowing, I glanced down, the outside of my right ankle, open, like a gargoyle's mouth, spurting, gushing blood. In the *moment* I was both *awareness* (the observer) witnessing the situation, and me, the actor in it, no script in hand. I've experienced this on a few occasions. In this situation once I surrendered to the experience, I was able to be in it without judgement and though it was bloody, bizarre and my well-trained nervous system had to put some effort in. I did question whether the absence of pain was down to my daily Kundalini Yoga practice genuinely strengthening my nervous system or whether the glass cutting to the bone had severed the nerves. Either way I sensed a beautiful freedom and was able to see and act with clarity. Why should this moment be any less beautiful than any other?

I guess I'd landed a role I hadn't auditioned for. As mentioned, I wasn't given a script, but I was given outlines to the situation. I realised it was down to me how I wanted to experience the moment and quickly became the scriptwriter. So, how do I want to feel in this moment? Am I putting my practice into action? Can I simply surrender and trust the *flow*?

As all this was playing out in my mind, I squeezed the flesh together and flung my leg on the counter... attempting to reduce the bleeding. I had to remind myself to breathe.

Breathe deep. My breath is my mantra, listening to its gentle purr, sensing the expansion and contraction throughout my body. Its waves ripple through me like water in a lake the moment a pebble is dropped in. In perceived challenging circumstances the simple act of returning to the breath can be forgotten.

The store manager brought me a chair, leg still raised on counter, we tied bandages super tight to halt the bleeding, she was very efficient, but I sensed stress. If one can't be present in so called normal situations, then how can one be conscious in an extraordinary occasion? I also became aware of the adrenaline running through my body, I started feeling incredibly cold, I'm still not sure why but I asked for a banana and some water.

Fluid, no resistance, I could've but wouldn't that go against nature's way? Do the plants growing along the river route fight growth? Do the birds struggle or look clumsy when the wind blows? No! Then why should I? Just because I've been raised in a time and space on this earth where drama, conflict, struggle, striving, dis-ease, dis-trust and fear have been etched into the fabric of society, why should I conform to that? Because subliminal programming is subconsciously fuelling those behavioural patterns? Taking us further away from a sense of connection, integration, oneness and love. Obviously, the situation wasn't ideal, but I trusted the path of ease would be more enjoyable, regardless of circumstance. Surrendering felt like I'd fast tracked to a Zen state... the eternal now. Though, *moment* by *moment,* seven hours in A & E did feel a little frustrating. None of the usual distractions I'd have in my bag, not even headphones, a book, lip balm... nothing. My phone wasn't a great distraction as the battery was fading. I had acquired the bananas and a bottle of water, what else did I need? I'd popped out for thirty minutes with no intention of having such an eventful day. So repeatedly compelled to surrender, I observed the waiting room...

One thing I've observed is, when things are perceived to be out of our control, we have a choice in how we respond. In stillness lies a deep connection to the *Divine* universal energy, when we are receptive and allow, it will always support us. If we trust it and our own intuition. Are they separate? Quite possibly not! Considering all knowledge is readily available, we simply need to decide which frequency we want to tune into... I digress.

I'd been thrown out of my comfort zone once again. I'm slowly realising it's when we are out of our comfort zone and in the beautifully chaotic playground of life, we somehow find a way, when *aware* it's a route filled with hyper synchronicities and beauty. Water always finds a way, sometimes crashing waves in a turbulent and overpowering manner other times with a delicate, soothing, graceful, divine *flow*.

Routines astray, I became aware of opportunities I may have previously overlooked. Hidden gates in magical gardens suddenly visible, a newly found courage backed by my soul to step out of my own way and walk gracefully into the unknown with an open heart, a sense of wonder and deep trust. I don't need to disclose how the rest of that day unfolded; the undercurrent washes it ashore. The effortless process is of experiencing the *Now*. Witnessing infinite subtleties in and throughout, allow us to truly experience the Divine within and all around. It is that simple, but since we've been conditioned to the opposite extreme and generally go about our day unaware with a finite attention span, it can be a little tricky to execute.

Present, in this moment take a breath, immerse yourself in it, observe entirety with a delicacy of awareness, listen with your heart.

"Instead of asking who has realised or what God is why not give your whole attention and awareness to what is? Then you

will find the unknown, or rather it will come to you. If you understand what is known, you will experience that extraordinary silence which is not induced, not enforced, that creative emptiness in which alone reality can enter. It cannot come to that which is becoming, which is striving; it can only come to that which is being, which understands what is."

J. Krishnamutri, *The First and last freedom, pg.* 265

~ *Divinity Speaking* ~
BE

Be Brave
Journey, No Judgement,

Breathe
Be
With A Delicacy of Awareness

Be

In being
Divinity Flows

Be
Trust Heart

ABOUT THE AUTHOR

SUZANNE NICHOLE PRESTON

Suzanne Nichole Preston is the founder of Bliss in Chaos. Using movement, meditation and breath practices, Suzanne coaches time-limited individuals and those wanting to take ownership of their wellbeing to reconnect mind, body and spirit. She focuses on creating a strong, flexible body and a calm, clear and focused mind to enable clients to navigate the chaos of urban life & empower them to live with *ease, power & fluidity*.

Influenced by a life of dance, twenty two years teaching Yoga and Pilates, and a deep exploration of embodiment disciplines including Somatics, Chi Kung, and Kundalini technologies, she incorporates her wealth of knowledge in a very accessible way.

Suzanne is also an actor and is often working on creative projects. She is currently developing The Urban Alchemy program.

Website: www.blissinchaos.com

Instagram:@suzanne_nichole_blissinchaos

Instagram: @blissinchaos

Email: suzanne@blissinchaos.com

22

LET YOUR INTUITION LIGHT YOUR WAY

TAMMY BRASWELL

"...And as we let our own light shine, we unconsciously give other people permission to do the same..."

— MARIANNE WILLIAMSON

We all have a guidance system that lights our way and when we allow ourselves to trust it, it helps us to shine our light brighter in this world.

But we often forget to tune in and trust it to the level that it is available to us...although when we do...life becomes so much easier to navigate and enjoy.

When I really opened up and embraced the divine being that I am and the Source of all things that I am connected to, the guidance and inspiration I receive changed.

I share this with you to inspire and remind you to let your intuition light your way, because you have so much to share when you do.

I've been experiencing energy, spirits, and even other planes of existence since I was a young child. I remember as far back, at least clearly, to the age of four, and everything I experienced felt normal to me.

It felt true to me although when I'd look out at the world and the people around me, they weren't talking about similar experiences for themselves. I knew on some level that what I was experiencing was not ready to be shared, so I went through life without sharing my experiences with anyone else until I was thirteen years old.

My parents divorced that year and my mom and I moved into our own place. This new environment with just the two of us opened up an experience that we shared, of mom's younger brother visiting us as he died a couple of months before I turned four in October 1973.

It was an interesting experience. His energy passed through both of us and for me, as it moved through the center of my body, it felt warm and cool at the same time. It was a pleasant, calming feeling like he was sharing his love with me.

After experiencing my uncle's presence with my mom, a new space of communication opened up for us. She shared experiences she had throughout her life that were similar to mine. I felt a deep relief to have my mom to talk to about what I had kept to myself for so long.

Several years later on December 12, 2016, which was my seventeenth birthday, my mom's dad transitioned from his body after the stroke he had two days earlier. Growing up I spent every summer with my mom's parents and was close to them, so his death on my birthday sent me into a tailspin of emotions.

His death prompted a two-week period where I unknowingly had a spiritual and energetic upleveling that opened me up to a whole new level of higher connection and communication, beyond what I was previously experiencing.

It ended up taking me thirty plus years to understand that was what was happening at the time.

Looking back even earlier to my uncle's death just before I turned four, what I remember happening beginning as a young child seems prompted by that event too. Both my mom's brother and father's deaths catapulted me into new levels of my intuitive senses, communicating with spirits, and experiencing unseen realms.

After that, I started having so many more spiritual, metaphysical, and energetic experiences. It was all to lead me to where I am now.

Those experiences opened me up for my path to become even clearer.

Today, I naturally and easily follow my intuition in my life and business to experience a higher way of living that I consciously create.

By tuning in and trusting my intuition and higher guidance, it steers me to choices that turn out better because I listen. And, in those moments when I don't listen...well they don't turn out how I prefer.

Now, I listen and sometimes don't even realize I am listening when things happen in the instant of a moment. Because I am so open and tuned in to that divine part of myself and All That Is, it just happens for me...and I listen and respond to it.

There have been significant times when listening, or not listening, to my intuition and higher guidance has reminded me why I do.

During the summer of 2003, my son was nine years old and we signed him up for the YMCA summer camp. Being a single working mom, he spent his summer days there.

He had gone there the summer before and I felt he was safe enough there, but this summer, I felt different. I had a sick feeling in my stomach when I thought about him going.

I can't explain how I receive my intuitive messages, but I knew that if he went to the water park they had planned, something would happen to him.

Trusting my intuition, I arranged to take the summer off of work and keep him home with me.

I felt confident with my decision and the sick feeling I had went away. Unfortunately that summer, there was a little boy who drowned at that water park and was from a YMCA camp.

It was sad to hear, but I knew because I listened to that inner nudging not to send him, he was safe.

The added bonus was that I started my own cleaning business that summer so he could be with me while I worked. Even better things came out of me following my intuition in this case.

In 2008, I had a different experience when not listening to the guidance of my intuition.

I was having computer issues and, although I'm good with technology, I wasn't sure if I could fix it. I had an inner knowing that I should not take care of this myself, but I went ahead and did a reset. I didn't realize the depth of my system it would go into, and it ended up wiping most of my computer clean, including a lot of important information and files.

Even as I pressed the button to set it in motion, I could feel I needed to stop, but I thought "how bad could the outcome be?"

It turned out to be worse than I thought. It caused me all kinds of stress and I ended up taking it to a computer repair place anyway. They were able to salvage a bit of my information, but not all of it and some important information was permanently lost. So, not listening to my intuition that time reminded me again why I do.

We've been taught that the sixth sense is the unusual one.

But what I've come to know is that it is the five physical senses that are the unusual ones because we are spiritual beings having a human experience, so that sense of knowing and receiving higher guidance is what is really 'normal' for us.

We are a soul on a human journey for the physical senses, contrast, emotions, and thoughts that can only be experienced in this physical plane. Because of that, our sixth sense of intuition is natural for us to access and utilize as a way to guide us in this physical plane with more ease and flow on our journey.

Our soul knows all is well and the truth of who we are here, but the human part of us goes into fear and forgets that. It functions from a limited field of awareness until we 'awaken' on our spiritual journey here, remembering who we really are and opening up to that truth.

Each of the five physical senses has an energetic sense associated with them and they are referred to as the 'clairs' including clairvoyance (higher sight) and clairaudience (higher hearing).

Those are what connect us to who we really are, not the limited five senses of our body, although our soul enjoys those for the fullness of the experience they offer here in the physical.

My business now, which is the expression of my divine purpose here, is based on using my intuition and clear connection with higher guidance that flows through me. I actually channel All That Is, which is Source energy itself.

It allows me to guide my clients along their journey in the highest ways and to help them process, heal, and release that which is no longer necessary energetically for the version of who they want to be now.

I've gotten to a place where I truly and completely trust my intuition and the higher guidance I receive for myself, those close to me, and my clients.

Back in 2011 when I began to offer my energetic and intuitive healing and coaching services, I didn't always or easily trust what I was receiving because it seemed unusual or I would censor it and only share what I thought a person would believe.

However, I found that what I received, even when I tried to hold parts of it back, would come out in the conversation because it was what was perfect and needed at the time.

So much has come through and been confirmed by others when I share it, so I know it is coming from a higher source of information.

There is also no way that I can know what I know and share. I often say that "I can't make that sh*t up" because it is so accurate and spot on.

The information I share with clients about things that have happened, are happening, and are going to happen is just not possible for me to know any other way than the higher guidance flowing through me, so now I truly and implicitly trust it.

I used to be concerned whether I would receive the information I needed when I was working with a client, but I have ALWAYS received what each person needs and even more than that.

The energy work that helps them to heal old patterns, beliefs, and blocks that keep them stuck in ways of living that they want to be different, is truly amazing in how specific it is for each of them.

I tune in for my clients and I tune in for myself so I know the best next steps that can be taken to achieve the results we each desire.

By allowing higher guidance to support us through our intuition and the nudges we receive to make choices easier in our lives, we experience more of what we want and a life that is of our own design, rather than just going along with what others have told us is acceptable and the way it 'should' be.

I've had so many incredible experiences in my life because I decided I wanted them and followed my intuition that guided me along the way.

Of course, this isn't just something I can do. You can do this too when you imagine the life you desire and follow as the intuitive nudges guide you in the unfolding of each step along the way.

Like when I met Wayne Dyer during his visit to Detroit in 2013.

I saw that he was coming to the area and wanted to go but none of my friends would join me so I decided not to.

At the time, I was going to a spiritual center on Sundays and became friends with the minister. He asked one Sunday if I was going to see Wayne and I said that I wasn't. He then asked if I would like to and I said "well, yes."

He told me that the center was gifting a few tickets to those who would hand out flyers at Wayne's event. I said I would so I received a ticket for the low-priced seating in the back of the room that held 2800 people.

There were mid and premium priced seats as well. Of course, the premium ones were in the front near the stage where Wayne was going to be. I wanted one of those when I was thinking about purchasing a ticket for myself and I still wanted one.

About a week before the event, I started envisioning someone coming up to me and giving me two of the premium tickets. I didn't know how that would happen, but I could feel that it was possible, so I felt into it and went on with things.

On the day of the event, I rode with another member of the center. The minister wanted help bringing the flyers in, so he asked one of us to join him. He hadn't given us the tickets yet, so we were just holding our place in line.

She asked me if I wanted to go help or continue to stand in line and my intuition told me to stay there, so she went to help him.

I was standing in line with no tickets and suddenly I heard my name. It was one of my very first energy clients.

We exchanged pleasantries and she asked if I was in the VIP line. I said no and she asked if I would like to be. Of course I replied "YES!" and she showed me two premium tickets that she had and wanted to send to me but didn't have my address as I had moved since she was my client.

Not only was I receiving the two tickets I imagined, but she had decided they were mine when she received them. Had I not followed the nudging to be the one who stayed in line, I may not have met up with her to receive them.

Once in, I chose an aisle seat five rows away from the stage. I was so excited that I decided Wayne was going to come down from the stage to shake my hand and take a picture with me. Again, I didn't know how that would happen but I knew it would.

While waiting for him to come into the room, the human side of me started to question whether it would happen, but my inner knowing knew otherwise so I held on to knowing that it would.

He came in and went up on stage. I started to question if he'd come down like I was imagining but let that go. Sure enough, he stepped off the stage and walked down the aisle I was sitting on.

I stood up to connect with him and he took my hand, which after all the hands he had shaken, he noted how cold it was. I laughed because that was what he noticed.

I asked for a picture with him and he said he had to get back on stage, but he stopped and took one with me. I share it on my Facebook profile and website among the others that I have taken with inspirational teachers that I also wanted to meet, including Marianne Williamson.

It is because of these experiences, and so many more, that I trust my intuition and the higher guidance that I receive and flows so easily to and through me.

I know it is there. I know it will always be there. It helps me with my choices and next steps and I couldn't imagine my life without being tuned into and trusting it.

When I am unable to hear it, I know that I am in fear and although it is still there for me, I can't easily hear or receive it because I am closing myself off being in that low place.

If you find yourself in those moments of fear sometimes too, I've found that when I relax, take a few deep breaths, and let the fear go... my intuition comes in easily and clearly again.

I constantly receive energetic and intuitive downloads for new programs and events I offer. I trust what I'm receiving and act upon it.

I have so much fun sharing my clear connection with my clients. I help them know the next steps to take, understand themselves as the divine spiritual being having the human experience that they are, and help them to live the life they truly want to live.

My higher connection helps me guide them into becoming the highest version of themselves that they can be, that they want to be, and to envision a life that they didn't easily imagine before.

I am able to hold a high level of possibility for them to step into and experience their life the way that is available for them to be, do, and have everything they desire.

It is exciting, amazing, and always interesting the things that come through for my clients that support them in truly living a life that is aligned with their soul's truth and is expressed in the elevated level of relationships, health, success, abundance, and spiritual growth they experience when we work together.

When you are given a space of possibility, so much opens up for you and I truly love assisting others in experiencing that.

Sharing energy work and the ways I am able to work with my clients brings such joy and fulfillment into my life. The space we share together is always fun, goes deep, and you never know what may come through for the betterment of all our lives.

I believe this is an amazing journey our soul chooses to take in this playground we call life and I know the life I have lived in my 52 years here wouldn't be as incredible and magical as it has been if I didn't listen to my intuition the way that I do.

What have you experienced by tuning into YOUR intuition and how has it guided you in your life?

~ Divinity Speaking ~
"Remember...you are the bringer of light wherever you are and wherever you go, so let your intuition light your way and you'll be living your divine purpose while you are here."

ABOUT THE AUTHOR

TAMMY BRASWELL

Tammy Braswell, international bestselling author, is The Vibrational Goddess of Create By Vibration LLC.

She supports emotionally, intuitively, and energetically sensitive women to heal their past and align with their soul's truth so they clearly create the life THEY choose to be living now.

By helping her clients shift into higher vibrational frequencies, they create their desires quickly, easily, and in alignment with their soul's desired human journey.

Being sensitive to energy, spirits, and other planes of existence since she was a child, her work as an intuitive channel, high vibrational healer, Akashic Record expert, and Energetic Creation coach and teacher is the expression of her divine purpose.

Tammy lives in SE Michigan with her pet aloe plants, enjoying healthy, organic foods while still having her favorite treats, and unapologetically watching mystical, magical and supernatural shows.

Website: www.createbyvibration.com

Facebook:

www.facebook.com/createbyvibrationwithtammybraswell/

Facebook Group:

www.facebook.com/groups/yourspiritualjourneyplayground

The Higher Consciousness Circle:

http://thehigherconsciousnesscircle.com

IT BEGINS WITH A FEELING

TARA HAISLIP

J'm a storyteller. I like to share my experiences as a way for others to feel less alone. In this space, I will try to convey a spiritual journey that started with so much toxicity but morphed into a life of groundedness by learning to trust; my heart, my intuition, and the Universe. I invite you to take what speaks to you and leave what doesn't.

When I reflect on where I am now compared to where I was fifteen years ago, it's overwhelming how much divinity, as I'll often say the Universe, worked through me. Yet, in the moment I felt lost like I was wandering through a thick fog trying to get to the other side of where I was. Fifteen years ago, I was very goal-oriented. I put all my energy into reaching a goal at all costs. The goal was my dance career. The cost was in the payment of sleep, peace of mind, monetary expenses, and my time.

I was a live wire of raw nerves running on five hours of sleep, working 2-3 jobs, in school full-time, and trying to make it happen. I was twenty-one years old finishing my degree at an art university in Philadelphia. I'm not from Philadelphia but I knew the moment we drove into the city for my audition that this was the school and city I wanted to attend. I felt it in my gut, my intuition, I was getting into this school.

THE TOXIC START

I was seventeen years old when I started college; living like I was on my own. My university had only one upperclassmen dorm where you paid $200 to enter the lottery for a room. I decided to forgo entering the lottery for one of the rooms after Freshman year and searched for my own place. I had my first apartment at eighteen years old. When it comes to the reality of your first place, the shine wears off when the bills start rolling in and you've wiped out your savings during Freshman year.

I eventually became used to the bills with minimal anxiety. I also became used to moving every year once my lease was up due to the 10-15% rent increase while only making $7.25 per hour at barely 25 hours per week. I learned to cut corners on basic needs like food and sleep. I did nothing to support my mental and emotional health. By the time I would graduate I would be a ball of nerves, sleep deprivation, and a walking black cloud. You'd usually see me with a cigarette in my mouth, coffee in one hand, big sunglasses on, and my headphones in along with the permanent resting bitch face. A complete joy to be around (totally being facetious). This exterior persona was a wall to keep people from seeing all that I was struggling with internally.

In my mind, I wasn't good enough for the career I chose which was essentially my life. I was constantly comparing myself to others and my self-talk was belittling me. I avoided being home in an attempt to avoid the massive void(s) in my life reflected in the emptiness of my apartments. The emptiness left me with only my thoughts. I sure as hell didn't want to be with those. I stayed out at all hours of the night with co-workers and colleagues partying, mainly drinking to numb my thoughts and emotions. In the beginning, it was common to party to network and build relationships. However, it turned into my escape by the end of college. It drove me deeper into my void until life felt bland without color and food had no taste. I felt lost in existence.

The toxicity of my thoughts and actions did two things: 1) Manifested into dis-ease, and physical pains within my body; and 2) Told the Universe this was what I wanted, so it gave me more. I struggled to land a dance gig. I was going to every audition I could get to from cruise lines to big and small dance companies within Philadelphia, NYC, and DC. My comparison game was on hyperdrive looking at the competition around me, telling myself I would never get the job. I was a shell of a person living solely for my career.

I willingly gave away my time which is the most precious commodity we all possess. By the end of the day, weeks, and months there was nothing left of me. Everything went into my dance career. I wouldn't stop pouring from my empty cup which was in deficit. Finally, my body made me stop and this was the turning point in my career. I had an audition in DC for which I rented a zip car to get myself there. I'm not sure I was supposed to drive it out of state but I did. I have many stories throughout my journey where I did things I probably shouldn't have. Those are stories for another time.

I get to my audition in DC. The audition director starts with the first plié combination on the right side of the body. As I did my grande plié in fifth position my right knee goes "pop, POP". Not entirely unusual for my knees but the second pop was a little loud. So much so, that it echoed in the studio with a resounding "eeww" from the other participants. Externally, I acted unfazed as I came up from my grande plié to finish the combination. Internally, I was freaking out.

I couldn't feel my quads, they had gone completely numb. Not just numb, I was having difficulty getting my muscles to respond. I continued through the three hour audition. The feeling in my muscles came back as though nothing had happened. I didn't get the job and headed back to Philadelphia in my zip car. On the way back I stopped at a rest stop to finally get something to eat for the day (I ate once a day, maybe). As I got out of the car, I struggled to completely bend or straighten my knee without shooting pains.

I remember trying to make myself walk normally without hobbling. I felt embarrassed that I had to hobble. I was gritting my teeth through the pain of walking while struggling with the idea of looking or being injured. I remember walking past the restrooms with the sounds of all the toilets flushing and thought "there goes my career". I got something to eat and I just sat there lost in what to do. My whole life was dance. Who was I now and what was I going to do?

So naturally, I ignored it and continued on like nothing was wrong with my physical, mental and emotional health. I continued to party to numb, avoided going home, and kept the toxic wheel turning. Eventually, I later learned that my meniscus got caught in my knee joint making it impossible to straighten or bend my knee. The knee became locked and permanently swollen. I had no choice but to head in for surgery.

THE SHIFT

In the chaos of everything that had transpired, I had a moment of clarity. It was like the fog cleared for a moment to help me see. It was a warm fall morning while I was laying in bed; the sun was filling the room giving it a warm glow. As I was staring at the ceiling, I was taking stock of my life and thought "this is not me, this is not my life, I don't want to be this person". It sounds trivial but it was more than thoughts; it was a feeling that vibrated throughout my body in the form of sorrow at the loss of myself.

The momentum from this moment propelled me toward a journey that reconstructed my life. I somehow intuitively knew that if I wanted to change my life I had to heal from within. The process didn't start with therapy, it started with a book. That book was You Can Heal Your Life, by Louise Hay. I had developed a routine of going to the local bookshop to find whatever spoke to me as a way to help me get comfortable with being with myself at home. One day, during this shift the book found me.

Based on that book, I started to practice gratitude for myself, my job, and my life as it was in the present moment. I would journal and say affirmations daily. Having never done this before, the practice felt strange. I felt silly saying things to myself on repeat. Although, it was comical when I'd be irritated at work, gritting my teeth while saying an affirmation to keep my smart mouth closed.

While I worked through the book, I had re-enrolled in school for paralegal studies. I really wanted work knowledge as well as book knowledge in this field. I included this aspect into my gratitude practice. The more I practiced the more I noticed the synchronicities happening around me, no longer thinking they were serendipitous. For instance, when I worked at a coffee shop, there were times when conversations would get louder at certain points or I would be at the right spot at the right time to hear a portion of a conversation that indicated a customer's line of work specifically in the legal field.

Eventually, I mustered up the courage to network by chatting with these customers about what they did, what firm they were with, and so on. It got to a point where I was doing this so often that my co-workers were taking notice. I was having fun trying to find my voice and confidence, again. I'd dealt with plenty of rejection in my dance career but this time I wasn't going to let it defeat me.

Don't get me wrong it wasn't all rainbows and butterflies. I got frustrated with the slow pace of the process. It felt like I was doing all of this work with no forward movement. However, I began to realize I was putting a lot of expectations on every conversation and job application. I worked on letting go of expectations to truly appreciate where I was in my life. I worked with some pretty awesome co-workers who made the job worth going to every day. I was making really great connections through school and excelling with a consistent 4.0 GPA each semester. My apartment wasn't great but it was perfect for what I needed at the time. It was like a little cubby I could hide away in to study and just be by myself. I was enjoying being in my own space with myself for the first time.

MANIFESTING BREAKTHROUGH

One day, job hunting per usual, I noticed an interesting craigslist job post. It didn't really say much about the employer but something about it pulled at me to apply. So, I did and then forgot about it until I had a voicemail to schedule an interview for what I thought the person said was the District Attorney's office.

On the day of the interview, I walked to the office address, went through the metal detectors at the ground floor, and headed on up to the 12th floor where I turned off the elevator to the entrance floor of the United States Attorney's Office (USAO). I was in shock and awe, maybe slightly wanted to pee my pants from nervousness. I signed myself in for the interview and sat down. Two people walked out, one of them would be my supervisor, who informed me that I would be interviewing in front of a panel of 12 people, 1-2 from each department, and they hoped I didn't mind. I wasn't intimidated at all during the interview, a little awe-struck, but everything felt in alignment. I just knew this was it. About two weeks later, I was offered the job of Student Clerk/Court Runner for the Criminal Division. It was the best first office job I could have ever manifested. I thought, well, damn, there is something to this manifesting, practicing gratitude stuff!

Once I got my job at the USAO I started to let my practice slip. Life was still pretty stressful trying to make ends meet. I was faced with how to stay in the city and my job. My position was contracted for the year I was in school. Once that year was up, I was out of a job. I was feverishly applying for GSA positions and with private practice firms.

My gratitude practice wasn't as grounded. It was a feverish plea to stay in the city or ask the Universe to help me stay. I ignored my intuition, I ignored the whispers which were all saying "it's time to go". Since I was being stubborn the Universe got stubborn. I was not getting any job interviews or leads.

I eventually decided to move to Virginia where I could live with my family to regroup. As soon as the decision was made, it was like the city started saying goodbye. The two weeks prior to my move, I would run into someone every day from a different point in my life during my time there. I was catching up with old colleagues and friends. It felt like I had a social life, again, which made leaving difficult. However, I did lean into the whispers that this wasn't a forever 'good-bye' but a sending off, the city would see me again, soon.

I moved to Virginia with a few hundred dollars and no prospects of a job. Within the first month I had three jobs. I worked for two law firms both part-time and a local coffee shop. The first year felt like a vacation. It's a resort-type area without the resorts. I started to meet people or be taken to events by my mother as a way to meet people. I met many who practiced in the holistic/therapeutic health field (massage therapy, Reiki, holistic therapy, so on). Many had their own businesses where they made, used, and sold their own products within their practices. This piqued my interest. I started to watch, listen, dream, and take part in their services. I wanted to learn more and be one of these people.

However, in true form, I got in my own way hell-bent on making it in my new career. It was more that I wanted to prove I could make it rather than a passion for being a paralegal. I never stayed with an office for more than two years. I was always searching for something more. Freedom. Freedom to be me without judgment or without feeling I needed to prove anything to anyone, not even myself. Freedom over my time and schedule; essentially to do whatever I wanted with my life. I didn't want to be chained to a desk living by someone else's schedule.

SHADOW WORK MAKES THE DREAM WORK

I left my paralegal career the same year I married, no longer able to stomach the lifestyle I had been living. About a year later I became serious about building my practice which the Universe soon took me on a condensed ride that was a mirror of everything I went through in my twenties. That condensed ride was a year of intense shadow work. It was absolutely terrifying to be facing similarities in my present life that I thought I had worked through. As I began re-working through each old but new situation, I realized I had not learned from my past. I had been running from it.

The flight or fight response kicked in at every synchronicity. I was facing knee surgery on my left knee, dealing with financial instability, working multiple jobs, housing instability, my marriage felt like an empty shell, but I had a small tribe in the form of two best friends who supported me through it all. This in no way discredits my marriage, we were both struggling with the long-distance that was our marriage. No matter how many times I wobble on this, my husband is my soulmate and always has my back regardless of what we are going through emotionally.

I always shied away from the term shadow work thinking that I didn't need to do it. The Universe said otherwise and I listened. I had to trust the process, my intuition, and stay grounded as much as possible. The true depths of the turning point I had been searching for 15 years prior was on the other side of this shadow work. The financial stability, housing stability, my marriage, general relationships, my body were all healing and coming back to me in bountiful ways. That momentum continues today.

We all experience these waves in our lives. I cannot count the number of times I've listened to others say I thought I worked through this, myself included. Whenever we're presented with those moments there is something we still need to learn. The more we lean into those moments the easier they get to navigate. Every experience is a building block to help us take on the next.

They can feel scary as you begin to recognize all that will change; relationships, networks, career. Take it day by day, one step at a time. Lean into the whispers of your intuition in the present to guide you. Trust in the process by letting go of expectations on the outcome. Reach out to those you feel pulled to connect with as they will lead to more of what you're looking to create in your life. As the old version of you begins to fall away, the new version can enter which includes new relationships, new networks, new careers, and most importantly, the you you've been looking for.

~ *Divinity Speaking* ~
"Self-approval and self-acceptance in the now are the keys to positive changes." - Louise L. Hay

ABOUT THE AUTHOR

TARA HAISLIP

Tara Haislip is a Lifestyle Wellness Coach, Spiritual Mentor, and the Founder of Grounded Energy111. Over the past 5 years, Tara has been a confidant to high-level career women working to break free from going through the motions of their daily life by identifying key fears blocking them from achieving their dream life in career, finances, and relationships. She helps create a clear path for how to move forward so they can end the mundane daily cycle, come home to their authentic self and create a life worth living.

Tara spent 15 years learning to reconstruct her own life after her dance career ended abruptly from injury. She has been featured on podcasts, in blog articles, and written for an online weight care clinic. When she is not coaching, writing, or podcasting you can find Tara outside in her garden running around with her toddler and down by the waterfront.

Website: www.groundedenergy111.com

Instagram: @groundedenergy111

AN INFINITE WALK THROUGH THE STARS

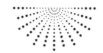

TERA NAMDEEP KAUR

*H*ello, Sat Nam. Divinity speaks to me in a variety of ways. I have found that I need the whole body "Yes!" to go forward on a project or idea. I have also learned that sometimes divinity speaks to me by telling me no, or not now, which is just as valuable. In my entire life, I have gathered knowledge, lessons, and teachings that have been waiting to have the lived experience before I shared them. I've tried to share them before but the timing was not right, I hadn't found the connection I was searching for to make a complete picture of what I was trying to have in a relay arts conversation with the universe.

A BIT ABOUT ME:

Astrology is as much of my Spiritual life as Kundalini yoga. I am not your typical 'woo-woo' gal. I am not a peace, love and light, softly-spoken person. I would say that I am 'tactfully blunt'. I am an odd duck that sees the bigger picture of Infinite. We are just a speck within a speck, within a speck, all on different frequencies of the

Universe. Not many of my close circle of friends or family totally get what I talk about or am interested in. They are supportive, but they just don't quite get it, and that's okay. That's why you become part of communities and find like-minded people for the support you need. Not a community to be in an echo chamber, but to express or just listen to others.

And yes, my writing voice is different from my video voice, and I have grown to love it. My writing brain allows me to articulate what my verbal brain may not be able to say. I don't do well with open ended questions, I need yes, no, maybe types of questions - it's how I'm built. I can explain in detail after I put it into a format of "have you ever" as compared to a "tell me a time" layout.

My interests are traditional astrology, kundalini yoga, tarot, natural majick, and the mind/body connection through mantra meditations. All of these require a certain amount of trust in your connection to Divinity and listening to what is being shared. I haven't always been so deeply connected to the Divinity Source as I wanted to be. I allowed life and self-doubt to get in the way, I thought I was just trying to reach for stars that weren't mine and I should be content just living a normal regular life. But *something* kept telling me that I needed to share what I had learned and share that voice. I had to wait until I made the connection to heart, mind, body, and Spirit and not let it just escape to the Ethers. Because when Divinity speaks to you, you can pull it down from the etheric realms and start again, and that is where I am now.

HOW I ARRIVED AT THIS POINT IN MY LIFE:

Through my online community connections at about 2015-16, I started having an overwhelming desire to learn astrology. I wanted to learn the roots and history, and more than just the psychological modern aspect, I wanted the art and science of the divinatory meanings and messages. When listening to my favorite astrology podcast they had a guest on and his message clicked, and his 'sermons from the stars' intrigued me.   Even though I considered myself a witch since I was thirteen, when he referenced the bible (he was a preacher's kid... his words, not mine) I would feel a resistance to the organized religious dogma associated with it.   And I began to ask myself, why? What was the resistance to hearing another viewpoint? I was okay with the other spiritual books he used and loved the teachings he referred to and decided I needed to work with that.   I even sent him an email telling him how much I enjoyed his videos and joked about my conflict but that I was happily going to work through it.   He is now a Bhakti yogi, and I looked into that practice but it didn't quite hit home. Many things resonated but again, *something* was telling me there was more to explore - so I did.   I looked into Kundalini yoga and it piqued my curiosity, but again..... *Something* told me I wasn't ready for it **yet**. So, I kept going forward, living my life, and absorbing information.   In 2020, I enrolled in my first Astrology course for Hellenistic Astrology with the former mentioned astrologer and became certified through the course. And I am currently taking two more courses concurrently to deepen my knowledge.

This brings me to about 2018, minor backtrack here... or retrograde if you will... and I am again introduced to Kundalini yoga, Guru Jagat specifically. I have never met her personally, but have met part of her wonderful family and this was how I found out about her. This connection turned my world around to say the very least. The connection to Infinity, Divinity, and Finite was made! Everything that I had been searching for was making a direct connection to me. When Guru Jagat passed on August 1st 2021, I had the most profound cathartic moment of my life, and I still don't know exactly why, other than, in retrospect, it was a change in the collective consciousness and frequency of a great voice being lost on this level on the planet Earth.

So, this takes us to the present moment, and my life path; my dharma, what I was sent here to do, and that is to share with people that they can work with the stars, planets, and your mind, body, and heart to connect with the Infinite voice of Divinity. You can work through rough transits and use the aspects to go beyond what you feel is holding you back or keeping you in a constant state of fear, worry or doubt.

If more people listened to their highest mindset, and enacted their neutral mind, instead of the negative personal self-talk of not being good enough, feeling lost, or overwhelmed; then the frequency on the planet would feel so much better for it. The ease of hearing Divinity speak to you can help guide you to where you want to be in your life. This can be done by mantra meditation (massive fan of this because I need the sound current, **Naad**, to guide me on a daily basis), physical activity, hint hint... Kundalini yoga is excellent for this, and exploring your natal birth chart and the transits that are happening and where and how Divinity is speaking to you through them. We live on a polarity planet, and that is more than just a spiritual philosophy. We have a magnetic north and magnetic south, so this planet has extreme opposites of positivity and negativity. What we need to do as a collective is come to a more neutral understanding. What empathy you have for the people closest to you needs to be shared with the world as a whole. No judgments, just understanding and a way to help and serve others. And I'm not saying everything has to be perfectly balanced and smooth going in your life. It is to understand the tensions of the moments and hold them, without letting them consume you.

HERE ARE SOME OF THE WAYS DIVINITY SPEAKS:

Almost every day I get information sent to me and I am recognizing it more than I ever did before, and it's because I have been listening with a more focused mindset. I will think about something I want to have an answer to and will begin by looking it up in a reference book, or some non-electronic paperwork and see if I can find an answer. Sometimes I find it, sometimes I don't, and then later that evening or the next day I will go online for something unrelated and I will find more answers to my original thoughts. And I have to say the majority of the time it is a Guru Jagat video, whether it was from years ago recorded before I even knew of her, or those up to her passing last year. If it is not her, it is one of my other mentors. I am always getting answers when I need them and that is divine. All I know is that I have found my spiritual home within this finite body. I know I can work within this energetic sound current to express Infinite wisdom through the stars. And I am meant to share it now.

INTRODUCTION TO ASTROLOGY:

The Moon placement in your chart represents the environment of what the plotline of the Sun's placement is going to give you direction, drive, or purpose too. And the phase of the Moon can express how the timing of these endeavors plays out. My Moon is in the third-quarter phase, so my whole life I have had a sense of urgency to accomplish everything, but I needed the experience first to accomplish my goals.

So, let's look at some traditional astrology. Do you know what it means if someone is talking about your big three? Or what your Ascendant is? Your big three are referred to as your Sun, Moon, and Rising Signs. These planets and placements give you and those around you a sense of who you are and how some of your personality traits may appear. The Rising Sign and the Ascendant are used interchangeably, but there are differences. The Ascendant is the exact degree the Sun was breaking over the horizon in the East. The Rising Sign is the House placement that that Ascendant degree resides in on the Chart Wheel. Most Natal charts you will see are formed into a circle. Some different areas of astrology can use a square or just a table layout, but for this purpose, we will talk about a chart wheel.

The Chart Wheel is divided into twelve topics of life, one for each House placement. Using the Whole Sign House (WSH) method, all twelve houses are laid out in equal thirty-degree sections. The first house is the only one that is specifically about you and how you are present in the world and how others perceive you. The other eleven topics represent a topic of your life, some are in the private sector and others are in the public arena. Houses one through six are your personal, or private sectors. Houses seven through twelve are public areas. Everyone has the twelve houses in their chart, and everyone has all the planets in their chart. You may have a house that is empty, meaning there are no planets in that house. And depending on how much you want to explore you may find you have asteroids, midpoints, or other aspects in a house. But for now, we will stick to the basics of traditional astrology.

HOUSE TOPICS:

1st – You, how you present to the world.

2nd – Your personal finances, how you create resources.

3rd – Your local community, lower levels of school, local travel or the idea for long distance travel.

4th – Home, family, father/parents.

5th – Creativity, children, sex, art, creation.

6th – Service, war, sickness or injury, servitude, small animals.

7th – Relationships of all types like marriage or business.

8th – Other people's money, death, taxes, inheritance.

9th – Higher learning, esoteric arts, long distance travel, religion.

10th – Career, what you practice.

11th – Friends, social groups and communities.

12th – Things that are hidden, reflection, suffering, dangers, escapism.

To take this to the next step, depending on your Rising/Ascendant sign, determines who Rules your chart placements. I am a Rising Libra, so that becomes my first house placement. Venus is the Ruler of Libra, so she becomes the Ruler of my Birth Chart. Scorpio is my second house, Sagittarius is the third house, all the way around zodiacal order until you get to Virgo in the twelfth house. Each of these zodiacal signs is ruled by one of the seven visible planets in traditional astrology, Uranus, Neptune, and Pluto were not considered because they could not be seen with the naked eye, and weren't discovered until many centuries later with the aid of telescopes.

WHO ARE THE RULERS OF THE ZODIAC?

Sun – Leo

Moon – Cancer

Mars – Aries and Scorpio

Venus – Taurus and Libra

Mercury – Gemini and Virgo

Jupiter – Sagittarius and Pisces

Saturn – Capricorn and Aquarius

How the planets act in certain Houses depends on if they are in their home sign or how they are in an aspect to other planets. If not in their home sign it is like being a guest at someone's home and depending on whether you like the house you are in it could be an easy time or a more difficult time. Each planet I consider to be like a demi-god and have lessons and transmissions to teach us. They are not to be used in a flippant way or just be used to "get" something. They are a vibrational expression of the Universe. All have different frequencies and sound currents to share if we take the time to listen to what they are saying. Astrology is like asking the Oracle, or Divinity, what wisdom it has in store for you and how to work through all that is given to you.

Traditional astrology also uses what are known as Dignities, which are the Modes: Tropical, Solid, and Double Bodied. In modern astrology, they are referred to as Cardinal, Fixed, and Mutable. It is how the energy of the demi-god is expressed. ***Tropical*** – Initiating, ***Solid*** – Stable, ***Double Bodied*** – Changeable. The Elements: ***Fiery*** – Intense and animated, ***Earthy*** – Practical and rigid, ***Airy*** – Moveable and communicative, and ***Watery*** – Fluid and receptive. This gives you the first clue as to how a particular sign personality behaves, like a Gemini rising person, is changeability in their action and speaking. Compared to a Taurus rising person who can be stable, practical, and more rigid in their approach to ideas. Or Mars is a Fiery Tropical sign, it likes to initiate action in projects or ideas.

Modalities of the Signs:

Leo: Solid Fire

Cancer: Tropical Water

Gemini: Double Bodied Air

Virgo: Double Bodied Earth

Taurus: Solid Earth

Libra: Tropical Air

Aries: Tropical Fire

Scorpio: Solid Water

Sagittarius: Double Bodied Fire

Pisces: Double Bodied Water

Capricorn: Tropical Earth

Aquarius: Solid Air

HOW I CONNECT KUNDALINI YOGA TO ASTROLOGY:

In Kundalini Yoga there are the Tattvas: Earth, Air, Fire, Water, and Ether (Spirit) which are the five elements that you are made of, and it is up to you how you handle yourself to keep these elements in a neutral position. The definitions for each of the Tattvas is much harsher than just the elements in astrology, but again, we live on a polarity planet and we are meant to find and hold the balance of the tensions of what is presented to us. Using the sound currents of mantra meditation and kriyas (yoga sets) helps you to stay neutral and be able to listen to what Divinity is telling you.

Tattvas:

Ether: Akasha Tattva – Your Throat chakra area; the Sound Current; Being steadfast.

Negative – A big ego; Positive – Realizing you are part of the Infinite.

Air: Vayu Tattva – Heart chakra area; Sense of Touch; Being balanced and unselfish.

Negative – Attachment to possessions; Positive – Serving others.

Fire: Agni Tattva - Naval chakra area; Sight; Being direct and not giving up.

Negative – Anger; Positive – Redirect the anger to work on your negativity.

Water: Apas Tattva – Root chakra area; Taste; Engaging.

Negative – Lust; Positive – Don't objectify people, use the energy to be of service to others.

Earth: Pritvi Tattva – Nonspecific chakra area but are the bones, flesh, skin, and teeth; Smell; Accommodating.

Negative – Greediness; Positives – Be of a higher caliber person.

MESSAGE TO YOU

I'm here to share that sometimes you need to have lived experiences before you are ready to share with a broader audience compared to just your close-knit circle and immediate environment. But it all starts with you and within you, and listening to what Divinity has to say. There have been times that I started endeavors, but knew something wasn't quite right with either the topic or the timing. I chalked it up to inexperience, or was I just not trying hard enough? Was I not meant to do more with my life other than the mundane everyday taking care of the daily business of life? And yes, at times I didn't push myself in the right direction. I took the easy way out, or my moderately severe depression and anxiety I wasn't recognizing took over. I had even gone from the end of work week drinks to drinking three to five times a week to numb out. I was overweight and just not in a good place in general. And as a side note, because of kundalini yoga, I no longer have depression or anxiety. I know I can meditate and chant a mantra to get me back into focus and a neutral mind. And I hardly drink anymore, maybe a few drinks every few months with friends, not alone, or out of trying to be numb. I've also lost over twenty-five pounds and am actually happy as a person. I've also come to realize those times in life were the times Divinity was telling me experience over expression. Get the experience now so you can express it with wisdom later.

~ Divinity Speaking ~

"Divinity Speaking has many levels to how She approaches us, but She can talk with us through astrology and we can connect to the Infinite while being in a Finite body, it is how we can connect to communities and heal on a collective level."

ABOUT THE AUTHOR

TERA NAMDEEP KAUR

Tera Namdeep Kaur is the Founder and CEO of Tera Namdeep SPC, a Social Purpose Corporation that focuses on people over profit.

Tera Namdeep is a Certified Hellenistic Astrologer and Kundalini Yoga Teacher. Through these practices, she is able to connect with the Demi-Gods of the Stars and the Tattvas, also known as the elements of Earth, Air, Fire, Water, and Ether (Spirit).

It is in these ancient practices that all of Tera Namdeep's lifelong learnings of esoteric arts culminated and she saw the need to help other spiritual seekers find a way to work *through* transits in their lives. She helps her clients stop the mental chatter and get past their stopping points and fulfill or find their purpose in this lifetime.

Tera Namdeep has two amazing and wonderful grown children, two daughters-in-law, and a happy, joyous grandson. She shares her home with her dog, Shae, and her momma kitty, Smudge.

Website: www.teranamdeep.com

Instagram: @teranamdeepkaur

COMING OUT OF THE SPIRITUAL CLOSET

TISH MEEHAN

I have been gifted with many spiritual gifts in this lifetime. I am beyond blessed. I know that I am here to do great things to help heal the collective, to heal the wounded Divine Feminine, help raise the Universal Shakti energy, and to bring balance and healing to the Divine Feminine and Divine Masculine energies. Ultimately, I am here to shake things up by bringing healing and messages from Spirit to wake people up. When I tap into this potentiality and the role that I know I am here to play (you can check my astrology chart if you don't believe me–I did!) I feel a surge of energy moving up my spine, from below my root chakra, all the way to my crown and beyond. I know this is my calling and I can't wait to take the leap into my true potential.

I visualize myself on the tallest mountain, standing on the edge, my breath flowing easily. I feel energy pulsating throughout my entire being and I know that I am ready to take flight, to say, *Hey world! Here I am!* Then I look down over the side of the cliff and my breath catches in my chest. I feel myself beginning to sweat, heart racing. A deep sense of fear and dread slowly rises inside me as I realize that I am scared of heights. I am scared to jump. I am scared to take the risk of falling, of failing. So I don't leap. Instead, I stand there frozen, paralyzed. And shame washes over me.

LIVING IN THE SPIRITUAL CLOSET

I have lived in the spiritual closet for more than twenty years. I am afraid of my spiritual gifts. I am afraid of looking like the crazy spiritual lady that you see on tv that throws crystals at people going through problems or is waving sage around while chanting incoherently. I am afraid of being seen as someone who talks to Spirit, Guides, and Angels. I am afraid of showing up as a spiritual leader because it means that I have to walk my talk and no longer hide from it. I have chosen to stay in the spiritual closet because it felt safe in there; warm and cozy, like a familiar blanket. Yet, I am stifled in this paradox that I live in. I long to fully own and embrace my amazing gifts and to show the world who I truly am–a Divine messenger, pure channel, healer, and teacher. Someone who yearns for spiritual wisdom, teachings and tools to help the world move out of the darkness we are shrouded in. But I am beyond scared to share what I know and to show up as one of the leaders who stands up to help humanity. So I stay hidden in my own spiritual closet, opening that door a crack to whisper- *hey world, I have some gifts that I want to share with you.* And just as quickly, I snap that door shut as the fear washes over me, like a wave of heaviness that pulls me under. I continue to tip-toe out of the closet and into my own light and back in again.

Oh, and I am super angry at God. Did I mention that?

LITTLE TISH–AGE 4

When I was four years old, I had a very vivid imagination. I loved spending time alone, away from my two older sisters, playing in my room with my imaginary friends. I would stand on the end of my bed to make myself feel taller because my imaginary companions were so big. I can remember feeling the brightness that they radiated and the joy that I felt being around them. This was one of the times that I can remember feeling truly happy–being in my room, with *my* friends that no one else could see or hear. It made me feel special because they gave me a lot of attention and I felt *happy* that I could be myself. I named these friends after my favorite television show, the Dukes of Hazzard – Bo, Luke, and Daisy. There were three. They were my spiritual guides and I loved them. What stands out for me as I recall this memory, is how much fun I would have but more importantly how I felt like I was transported to another place and time. I can picture in my mind a big field where we would play. It had purple flowers and the grass was soft. The air was warm, but not hot. My imaginary friends and I would go there in the game I would create.

Then one day, my older sister decided to spy on me. I was talking to Bo and Luke, whom she couldn't see, when I spotted her face peeking around the corner. When I locked eyes with her, she began to laugh and make fun of me for playing with imaginary friends. The heat rose within me, my face burning red with embarrassment, tears in my eyes. I threw myself on my bed and buried my face, where I cried until the pillow was soaked with tears. I could hear my sister running through the house laughing and telling everyone about how I had imaginary friends. That was the last time I saw those imaginary friends. I wouldn't allow myself to see them or talk to them, even if they came by. I closed that door and refused to let it open because it didn't feel safe. I went into the closet. Angry and afraid of who I was and I pushed away the spiritual gifts that were emerging from my innocence.

AGE 14-DEVASTATION

When I was fourteen, my mom died suddenly. She had a heart attack in the middle of the night when the rest of us were asleep. We discovered her body the next morning. It felt as though my heart and soul were ripped into a million pieces. I spent the next few years lost in a sea of despair, darkness and depression. I was afraid all the time. I had to sleep with music on because the silence would swallow me alive. I struggled to connect with friends because no one really understood the magnitude of this hole that was inside me. I felt broken and didn't know how to put the pieces of myself back together. My emotions moved from being numb, to overwhelming sadness, to extreme anger - around and around it went with little or no relief. This anger was trapped inside of me and it burned deep in my belly. Anger at my mom for not taking care of herself better, for smoking, and for leaving me. Anger at the world for moving forward as if nothing had happened. Anger for the kids at school who were laughing, happy, and carefree. And a deep, deep, festering anger at God. I prayed that this was all a bad dream and that I would wake up and my mom would be back. I prayed for peace and solace for my broken heart. But nothing changed. I was still that lost teenager wandering through the halls at school, trying to remember how to breathe and put one foot in front of the other, praying that I wouldn't fall to pieces in front of everyone. Life seemed so empty and unfair, and I didn't want to live anymore. I tried to fill the void with friends, alcohol, boyfriends, and anything that felt good. Nothing lasted.

Over time, I learned to put a fake smile on my face. This mask made me feel safe and unseen, which was exactly what I wanted. I began to allow the people around me to guide my life, make decisions for me and my future because it was easier than trying to navigate my world without my mom. It was at age seventeen, that I met the guy that I would eventually marry. He took the reins of my life and steered me in a direction that felt safe and secure. I finally started to feel normal.

I was beginning to put the pieces of myself and my life back together and nothing would get in my way. The anger was tamed for now, the tears subsided, and I started to feel *normal*. I finally felt like things were turning around for me.

But there was a nudge inside of me. Something didn't quite feel right. I loved my boyfriend and felt safe. I felt really safe. Yet, something was still off. I chose to ignore that quiet voice inside that was saying, *Tish, pay attention.* I ignored it and kept pushing through. The need to be protected, safe, and content trumped anything else that showed up.

ANGER IGNITES MY PATH

And then things began to shift for me in ways that I hadn't expected. For my twentieth birthday, I received a gift certificate for a reiki session. I had no idea what it was and felt extremely put off by it. I tucked the piece of paper with the woman's name away inside a book, and forgot about it. A year later, when I was packing up my room to move, I found that piece of paper. This time I was met with a sense of curiosity and a longing that I couldn't quite understand. I made the appointment without realizing that this would be a pinnacle moment in my spiritual evolution. The reiki practitioner was very kind and normal, which was a surprise, not like the crazy spiritual people I had seen in movies and on tv. As soon as the session began, she began to channel my Guides and Angels. This woman knew nothing about me. NOTHING. Her words still sit with me, in my heart. A truth that still holds true to this day. "I can see that you lost your mom. You are so sad and lost. And you are angry. Angry at God for taking her away from you." As plain and simple as that. I was lost. Sad beyond words. And I was angry at God.

Many things ran through my mind that day. How did this woman know these things about me? Why did this feel so right, to be here, in her home, receiving healing that I could feel in my entire being? I knew right then and there that this was the beginning of my true healing journey. Little did I know that it was the beginning of my spiritual path to being a healer, channel, and teacher. This day also began the paradox in which I still find myself.

FAST FORWARD TO AGE 38

The years between that first Reiki session are peppered with so many beautiful moments, and many challenges. I got married, had three kids, and became an elementary school teacher. I was happy enough. My grief was buried deep inside me and I just kept moving through the weeks, months and years. I continued to receive healing from my reiki master and started to attend her weekly meditation classes. I didn't tell many people about this part of me because it felt personal. I loved learning about the spirit world and going there in my meditations. When I was meditating, I felt that I was finally understanding the world and myself. During this time, I became more aware of my emotions, sensitive nature, and I noticed more and more people coming to me for advice and an ear to listen. I guess I am what is called an empath. These traits became more and more evident the more I meditated and received healing. As an empath, I began to pick up other people's emotions and physical pain, and it was overwhelming. I struggled to know what was mine and what was someone else's. It was at this time when I decided to take my first level of reiki so that I could do self-healing and stay clear of other people's stuff. I wasn't expecting to feel pulled more into the spiritual world. I thought it was for me, I truly did. But something shifted in me, a light went on and I started to feel a calling to do more, to offer healing to others and continue to build my knowledge of the spiritual world and my role in it.

I took course after course, emerged in learning and healing. On one hand, it was incredible and I loved every second of it because I felt like I was in the right place. On the other hand, this new path created drama and issues in my life. My partner did not support this new part of me and thought I was a bit crazy. I couldn't articulate how things worked and why I loved doing healing work and self-healing, why I had crystals and cards, essential oils and pendulums. I began to question whether maybe I was crazy. I felt embarrassed and ashamed of my spirituality and so I kept it hidden. I would keep all of my spiritual paraphernalia in a little cupboard, only pulling it out when I was alone or with a few trusted people. I became unhappy. The more I hid this part of myself, the worse I felt. I began to hate my job, wanting to quit and follow my path as a spiritual healer. As my spirituality strengthened and the doors to new possibilities opened, the more I hid myself away in my self imposed spiritual closet. I felt like that four year old who talked to imaginary friends, who I realized were my guides, and an anger began to fester in me again. I was angry that God had shown me this path and I wasn't able to take it; that I had to choose between my marriage and my path. I tried to find ways to connect these two seemingly polar opposite parts of myself, but the more I tried, the more chaos would erupt in my life. My partner and I grew further apart. I was angry all the time, I had panic attacks at school, I had no energy for my kids and I was miserable. I begged my partner to support this new career but was met with resistance. I knew he was working from his own need for safety and security, but it didn't matter anymore. I would silently scream to my mom and my angels to help me find a way to make everything work. I was falling apart mentally and emotionally and felt like that broken teenager once again, lost in a sea of sadness and frustration.

At age forty, I knew that I had to make a big change. I had to follow my knowing and leave my marriage. To say it was the hardest thing I have ever had to live through falls short. Choosing myself and my path over my family – that is what it felt like, and still does. And here I am, a few short years later still figuring it out. Leaning into my gifts and slowly showing them to the world. I talk to my children about all things spiritual and even though it was hard at first, it gets easier. I want them to know this side of themselves. I continue to learn, devouring all teachings and wisdom that I can knowing that it is leading somewhere that I can't even imagine. I am learning to trust my voice, my knowledge, my intuition and I am healing the wounds that have kept me angry with my mom for dying, and the anger I have with God. I can trust Spirit and Universe, but the label God still stirs something in me. I am a work in progress, but I am finally feeling like it's time to step out of this spiritual limbo and into my own light. For myself, my children, my community, and for the collective.

A MESSAGE FROM SPIRIT

During the process of writing this chapter, I was met with a lot of resistance. So I asked myself, my truest, most divine self – why am I fighting this? What am I afraid of? And the answer rings out from the music playing behind me, "Here am I with the mighty and the high, feeling like I don't belong." Fears bubble up before my mind's eye, like a slideshow of all the ways I fall short. I feel like a fraud, a fake, an imposter. My fear asks me, who are you to call yourself a healer? A spiritual teacher? An author? Who are *you* to call yourself a Divine channel?!" This last part creates a reverberation throughout my being and I pause. I take a long inhale and focus only on my breath and the feelings that are present. I mentally ask myself, *What makes me think that what I have to say is important? Needed?* As I quiet the inner chatter of my ego through the strength of my breath, I surrender and allow the answer to come to me. It arrives as if floating on a cloud from the Divine to my heart. Spirit speaks to me, "I ask you, Dear One, who are you not to share your gifts with the world? How can you continue to dim your light so that you are barely a flicker in the sky? You are needed, now, in this moment to open yourself up fully and completely to your soul purpose. The collective needs you. Your family needs you. Your community is waiting for you to step up and into the light, to be a leader for those who cannot hear their own guidance and find the light." A vision appears before me of a domino, lit up in an ecstatic white light that is so brilliant it hurts my eyes. As I embody and embrace this light, the domino connects with the one beside it, and it lights up and pushes into the next one, lighting it to its brilliance. I watch as all the dominos begin to fall, one by one, lit to their fullest potential. I understand.

When I step into the light of the Divine, it helps others to find the light and live their most soulful life.

When I get out of my own way, I allow the Divine to move through me. It is effortless because I am in the flow. This is the place I am choosing to breathe into, to nurture, to challenge, and to trust. I choose to use any residual anger that comes up within me to be the fire that transmutes another layer of my being, like a phoenix emerging from the fire.

Again, I am standing on the edge of the mountain, my arms spread wide. I breathe into this new found confidence and self-assurance. I boldly and courageously leap.

I am ready.

Are you?

~ Divinity Speaking ~
"Divinity speaks when your heart and mind are open to listening. Have faith in the messages you receive and allow the Divine to speak to you, and through you."

ABOUT THE AUTHOR

TISH MEEHAN

Tish Meehan is a Transformational Soul Coach, Spiritual teacher and healer, and Divine channel. Tish helps women who struggle with chronic overthinking, are emotionally repressed, and feel silenced to take off their masks and connect to their inner, sacred fire to embrace their spiritual gifts, heal their trauma, and fully embrace their spiritual path to liberation. Tish believes that this is the time for the Divine Feminine to release deep seated wounding and barriers that keep women from healing themselves and the collective consciousness. Tish is an international bestselling author for her work in Ignite Your Wisdom, and shares her story of rising up into her own light in the book entitled Divinity Speaks. Tish lives in Toronto, Canada with her three children, two cats and a dog.

Facebook: @tishmeehanspiritualhealer

Instagram: @tishmeehan1111

Linkedin: www.linkedin.com/in/tishmeehan

ABOUT THE PUBLISHER

*B*ridget Aileen Sicsko is the founder of Exalted Publishing House, a podcast host and a visibility strategist. She helps successful entrepreneurs stand out and be featured as leaders in their industry by sharing powerful stories, writing best-selling books and gaining global recognition. Bridget believes in the power of words, stories and voices to shift our view of reality, our potential and our purpose on the planet. In addition, she considers herself a master community builder and has gathered hundreds of female leaders in her online community, mastermind program, networking events, and women's circles. Bridget also hosts a podcast called She Builds Empires. Bridget has been featured in Authority Magazine, Women's Business Daily, Thrive Global, The Medium, on Ticker News, News 12 New York and several podcasts. She lives in New Jersey with her husband and her border collie beagle, Finn.

Website: www.bridgetaileen.com

Instagram: @bridgetaileensicsko

Instagram: @exaltedpublishinghouse

ABOUT EXALTED PUBLISHING HOUSE

*E*xalted Publishing House produces books that move hearts and minds.

We are a hybrid *book publisher* for founders, leaders, CEOS, entrepreneurs and business owners who want to get more eyes on their story.

Exalted Publishing House has a simple philosophy: change the world through words. Our aim is to work with a small number of entrepreneurs, organizations and businesses each year to uphold the highest standard of intimacy and personalization in the cathartic writing and publishing process. We mainly work in the realms of the alternative, disenfranchised & different by sharing stories that aren't always spoken through mainstream channels.

Corporate Books

We create multi-author books for business owners, CEOS and organizations to highlight the stories of their mission, brand, teams and employees.

Multi-Author Books & Visibility Programs

We work with leaders and entrepreneurs who want to get featured in top tier publications and podcasts and share their story to elevate their brand.

Visibility on Purpose

Join a one-year long program to help founders and business owners get media ready.

If you would like to purchase a 100+ bulk order of any of our books for schools, organizations, teams, book clubs at a discounted rate, please contact bridget@bridgetaileen.com for details and prices.

Others Books by Exalted Publishing House

Legacy Speaks, Powerhouse Women Leading Lives Worth Remembering

Success Codes, Secrets To Success You Weren't Taught In School

Lineage Speaks, Women Who Carry The Torch For Future Generations

Where Social Work Can Lead You, Journeys Into Around and Even Out Of Social Work

Prosperity Codes, How To Attune To & Attract Wealth, Joy and Abundance

Coming Soon...

"Heart-Centered Leadership"